LITTLE BOOK OF
BETJEMAN

Written by Peter Gammond

Foreword

I am glad to be able to add my blessing to Peter's little book about John Betjeman, a man who was both a friend and an inspiration to me, for I know that Peter has a balanced view of him – love and admiration on the one hand, balanced criticism on the other. We have shared many pleasant occasions visiting the places he knew and enjoying reading and hearing his immortal works. This book sums it all up very warmly and wisely.

The Lady Wilson of Rievaulx

Mary Wilson

LITTLE BOOK OF
BETJEMAN

First edition 2006. Revised edition 2012

© G2 Entertainment Limited 2012

www.G2ent.co.uk

Printed and bound printed in the China

ISBN 978-1-907803-39-0

Contents

LEFT The Church of St.Enodoc,
Trebetherick, North Cornwall. A pivot of
the poet's life from early childhood days;
where he and his mother are now buried.

Introduction

The life of John Betjeman fits very neatly into the twentieth century. He was born in 1906 in the Edwardian age, a time often regarded – though possibly mistakenly – as a golden one and died 78 years later when Mrs Thatcher was in charge of things. At the time of his death this supreme English poet was one of the most popular ones of any age, respected and even loved by his peers, by his readers and by thousands of people for whom poetry was of no importance whatsoever. He had received numerous honours, was Poet Laureate and would soon be commemorated in the Poet's Corner of Westminster Abbey. He died a poet, something he had always wanted to be from his years as a boy on Highgate's West Hill when he also developed the strain of melancholy that haunted him all his life. Fortunately, Sir John earned and enjoyed a vast bonus of laughter and was blessed with many wonderful and valued friends.

Peter Gammond has written an excellent and much-needed account of the life and work of a most remarkable man. This is not an official biography – Bevis Hillier has already produced that – but it is a useful compact book enabling readers to understand something about Sir John and all he stands for.

Peter is eminently qualified for the job. A one-time chairman of The Betjeman Society he has played a vital part since its formation in 1988, ensuring that it met its aim of promoting the study and appreciation of Sir John. His editorship of The

Betjemanian, the annual journal, has certainly helped to do that.

Long before the Society was even thought of, however, Peter Gammond was fascinated by the poet. He had occasionally met him in Oxford, London and Cornwall, all significant places on the Betjeman map. He discovered that, for a while, he lived only a few doors away from Betjeman's childhood home in Highgate. He became a serious collector of his work – and of the hundreds of books and articles written about, or featuring, him. Most important of all, he reads and re-reads those works. Many people say they love poetry but they don't read it. I can assure you that that is not the case with Peter. I have seen his well-thumbed copies of the *Collected Poems*.

This book describes an extraordinary career and, chapter by chapter, details a full and sometimes surprising life. We meet Betjeman the film critic, the hugely productive book reviewer, the tireless champion of England and fighter for the preservation of the best of our architectural heritage and, of course, the man who became what is now called a celebrity – famous for being John Betjeman. We meet him always as a poet and see that poetry is present in all that he did.

The subject of this book taught us to look at what is around us. Without his influence there would be a gap in our lives. This is a story well worth telling.

John Heald
Vice-Chairman of Betjeman Society

LEFT The author and John Heald on a Betjeman-fishing trip to the pier at Southend which the poet helped to save. *Photo: Ann Heald.*

The Laureate

The most approachable and, for many, the most enjoyable of 20th century poets, is generally referred to in the reference books as 'Sir John Betjeman, CBE, Poet Laureate' which is all very gracious and grand but it does conjure up a rather formal picture of a person whose character was essentially informal, endearing and unworldly.

Betjeman, always a respecter of tradition, was very pleased to have the honours, as most people would be, even if he was rather embarrassed by them – for he was, on the whole, a modest man – and often felt burdened by the dignity and responsibility that it thrust upon him. The knighthood (a fairly rare accolade for a poet), which he received in 1969, was well-deserved and happily accepted. The Poet Laureateship, however, was another matter and, while he was delighted to hold the post, it was always a bit of a millstone, particularly when it came to having to write the sort of things that Poets Laureate are expected to write. The joyfully satirical quality of a typical Betjeman poem:

'Think of what our Nation stands for,
Books from Boots' and country lanes,
Free speech, free passes, class distinctions,
Democracy and proper drains.'

is what the multitude of Betjeman admirers find very much to their taste, but it

is not exactly in the official vein that some people might expect from a laureate.

At the time of his appointment it was generally agreed that JB was the best candidate for the office, but when it came to the crunch he was no better at writing official poems than most laureates had been before him or since. At one stage, during his tenure, he was told by Parliament and the press that if he couldn't do better he really ought to step down. But it was only the press who were really worried, for, in fact, the public always found him a true laureate of the people and continued to enjoy what he produced, while, to be fair to his employers, there was never any great pressure put upon him (or on previous holders of the position) to produce official odes and celebrations on demand.

The real honour that is offered is simply that of being in the same distinguished company as John Dryden, William Wordsworth, Robert Southey, Lord Alfred Tennyson (especially him), Robert Bridges and John Masefield. Although it is slightly tarnished by the fact that some of the other holders of the office included

THE LAUREATE

Thomas Shadwell, Nahum Tate, Nicholas Rowe, Laurence Eusden, Colley Cibber, William Whitehead, Thomas Warton, Henry Pye and Alfred Austin (especially him) – none of whom actually set the literary world alight.

When John Masefield died in 1967, Betjeman was considered by many to be an obvious successor but the honour went to the more austerely academic Cecil Day Lewis (even though he had once been a member of the Communist Party) and Betjeman had to wait for Day Lewis's death in 1972 before he succeeded to the title amid wide acclaim:

'Lucky old England's poet' wrote Philip Larkin in *The Sunday Times*.

'Almost uniquely qualified' said John Hollander in *The New York Times*.

'Most popular choice as Poet Laureate' said *The Daily Telegraph*.

'A new Poet Laureate – with magic' – Keith Brace in *Birmingham Post*.

And Osbert Lancaster summoned up the situation very nicely in a *Daily Express* pocket cartoon featuring two beefy sporting girls with the caption 'I say, Daphne, isn't it *super* about the new Laureate?!' Betjeman was then 66.

In 1984, when he died at the age of 77, *The Times*, in its usual anonymous and pontifical way, summed up his achievement. 'Few could be so rightly endowed for the role of Poet Laureate in the present age, even though his explicitly laureate verse was undeniably weak. He was a living repudiation of the idea that poetry must necessarily be arcane or saturnine, and though he had no more success than any other poet since the Divine Right of Kings fell into disfavour in celebrating royal weddings and nativities without bathos, he did celebrate, with the most lively specificity, a Britain that his readers could recognise and love, while applying a compassionate lash to some of its private and public faults. If the laureateship is to be something more than a gong for the eminent elderly bard, as it should be, and something like a role of National Poet, his approach is the one that a successor is most likely to find rewarding.'

"I say, Daphne, isn't it *super* about the new Laureate?!" 11.x.72

The Man

He was born on 28 August 1906, on the gentle slopes that lie between Kentish Town and the foot of the steeper Highgate West Hill, at 52 Parliament Hill Mansions; a red-tiled middle class block of buildings that hardly had the chance to contribute to his childhood imagination. The Betjemann family, third generation purveyors of high class household fittings, and then at a peak of affluence, left Parliament Hill Mansions when John was only three. They moved some way up the hill (as people improving themselves so often like to do) beyond St. Anne's Church (where he had been baptised in 1906) to 31 Highgate West Hill – a modest but stylish terrace house built when all of that area still looked out onto the green orchards that became the Burdett-Coutts estate in the 1930s. Betjeman developed a deep affection for this childhood home where he spent his crucial developing years up to 1917. 'Deeply I loved thee 31 West Hill' he wrote in his autobiographical poem *Summoned by Bells* in 1960.

When the family moved to Chelsea while he was away at school in Oxford he was greatly upset. It added to his growing alienation from his family – particularly his father Ernest Betjemann, a golfing, shooting and fishing sort of chap, probably a much kinder and more sensitive man than the poet sometimes portrayed him, who ran the family business in the Pentonville Road. The double 'nn' at the end of their name (which JB himself used on and off until his Oxford University days) was a clear indication of German origins and, indeed, much recent research has fairly firmly placed the family background in the Bremen area from whence one George Betjemann had emigrated to London around 1797. The family firm, specialising in upper middle class furnishings for affluent homes, selling to such outlets as Aspreys of Bond Street, had prospered partly through the invention and exploitation of the 'tantalus' – a device which safely locked up the sherry and spirits decanters out of reach of thirsty servants. Philip Asprey, the head of his family firm became a close friend of Ernest, played golf with him in Cornwall and went shooting with him in Norfolk where Betjemann Senior leased 800 acres of pheasant shooting land.

MIDDLE The poet revisits his childhood home at 31 Highgate West Hill.

BELOW The font where he was christened at St.Anne's Church, Highgate on 25 November 1906.

THE MAN

ABOVE The
fortunes of the
Betjemann business
were partly founded
on the success
of their patented
'tantalus'.

Betjeman's mother Mabel Bessie Davis was of pure British stock from a family well-rooted in and around Spalding in Lincolnshire and she, prompted by the strongly anti-German feelings that flourished in the years leading up to and during the First World War, tried to persuade John, and herself, that the Betjemann family was really of Dutch origin. It was Mrs Bouman, who lived next door at West Hill and whose children (including Bobby – who became the subject of the poem *Narcissus*) were his closest friends until they moved away in 1910, who was named by Betjeman in *Summoned by Bells* as the person who subverted him with the idea that they really were of German descent – though she later denied this. Meanwhile, however much John enjoyed its ambience and surroundings (and who could not enjoy Highgate West Hill on a sunny summer Sunday morning with the bells ringing and the birds singing, the squirrels a-leaping, and the band droning distantly from beside Highgate Ponds), it was a pity that No. 31 was not entirely a happy home for his father and mother quarrelled incessantly and John was often at odds with his father who always

LEFT 52 Parliament Hill Mansions where the poet was born in 1906.

expected him to think of joining the family business, and would drag him unwillingly away on the firm's outings to Norfolk and make him join in the shooting (at which he was completely hopeless).

From this middle class family and upper crust surroundings he inherited his slightly 'posh' accent and the tendency to use such pronunciations as 'gel' and 'goff', at the same time probably inheriting some of his intimate knowledge of the commercial brands of the time, with which he tellingly illuminated his poems, from a succession of servants, among whom he especially adored his nanny, Hannah Walker. He often read his poems to her and regularly visited her in her retirement in Tottenham to read his latest work for her approval. There was also a calvinistic nursemaid called Maud who was rarely nice to him and occasionally spanked him – with what dire results we can only speculate upon. 'Lying in bed of a late summer evening,' he wrote in 1951, 'I remember the bells ringing out from St. Anne's, Highgate Rise – the church where I was christened; they poured their sound, deep and sorrowful, over the Burdett-Coutts estate, through the hornbeam leaves I could see from the bed. And Maud, the nurse, was looking out of the open window. Crossed in love, I suppose, and, for once, fairly gentle with me. I remember asking her if I would go to heaven. 'You will, but I won't,' she said. And I remember recognising even then that she spoke from her heart about herself. I did not recognise this at the time, and I suppose I could not have done, as any sign of grace in Maud. Nor did I really believe that I would go to heaven, and still less do I think so now.'

In the endless term times the small, sad and introverted boy trudged daily up West Hill, weighed down by his double 'nn' and the nasty little bullies who would prance around him shouting 'Betjemann's a German spy' as he made his way to Byron House, his first school in Hampstead Lane (now gone), and later to Highgate

BELOW
Betjeman (left) with seaside holiday friends c.1914-16.
Photo: courtesy of David Engleheart.

ABOVE *Little Innocents* (1932) was a collection of childhood memories. Betjeman wrote about his Marlborough schooldays.

Junior School where his eventual friend Mr. T. S. Eliot (to whom he showed his poems without receiving any obvious encouragement) was then the English master. This portentous crossing of paths is now commemorated by a blue plaque beside the door through which he entered daily. Or else he was on his way to one of the endless parties in one of the big Highgate houses where, on an occasion he never forgot, one tactless lady was heard to say that she thought him 'a rather common little boy'. Or daily where he caught every possible glimpse of his heart's desire – a tall, bouncy, blue-eyed, golden-haired girl called Peggy Purey-Cust who lived at No. 82 and gave him no encouragement at all. He later sighed sadly that all his later loves had something of Peggy Purey-Cust about them.

Highgate was redolent of the names of poets from Coleridge to Houseman who had lived and written there and, knowingly or not, Betjeman always felt certain that, whatever his father and Mr. T. S. Eliot thought, he was going to be a poet. He would wander into Parliament Hill Fields and look out over the London, less cramped and crowded then, which he described and mourned for in so many of his poems. He liked to think that the passing citizens would be saying to themselves 'oh, look, there's a poet!' At least Parliament Hill Fields was 'country' of a sort with fields and trees and distant aspects and, although Betjeman was undeniably a Londoner and lived most of his working days there, he was for ever longing for the country – loving Norfolk in spite of his father, loving the White Horse country where his early married homes were, and, acquiring a deep love for Cornwall where the family went for their regular summer holidays in Trebetherick, down the River Camel on the other side of the estuary from Padstow.

A large part of his work was inspired by the colour and character of the places he loved or lived in. He would get to know, with un-boyish diligence, the living details and the long history of such places so that his writings were steeped in the true colours, sounds and scents which he would then accentuate by comparison with the people who disported themselves there – the snobby little children on the beach at Daymer Bay, the horsey folk of Lambourn, the City business girls, the hoardings and adverts that clashed with historic backgrounds, the crazy rush of modern life, and the quiet comfort of churches which he enjoyed, as he once said in a TV interview simply because they were there, 'always the same' whatever was happening in the world outside.

In a clearly predestined, but then unpremeditated, sequence of events, we

BELOW Surveying his old domain from Parliament Hill Fields where he sat as a boy hoping passers-by would say 'Look, there's a poet!'

THE MAN

BELOW One of the first churches he found and admired in Cornwall – St.Protus & St.Hyacinth in Blisland on the fringes of Bodmin Moor.

now find Sir John Betjeman, CBE, Poet Laureate, at rest in an untidy plot in the compact graveyard of one of the smallest and remotest churches in the country: the church of St. Enodoc in the parish of St. Minver in North Cornwall. A simple rounded headstone made from local Delabole slate, is inscribed in the fanciful style of lithography that he showed a liking for in *Mount Zion* and other early books. After 20 years the grave still has an untended look, lonely in a dusty patch of earth with usually, at most, a jam jar with a few local flowers wilting in it. The once

LEFT Architect Sir Ninian Comper (1864-1960) [right] the restorer of Blisland Church, and a Betjeman idol.

surrounding grass has long given up the struggle against the sturdy footwear of the devoted and the curious who come to gaze on this modest monument. 'You must see this place,' a passing lady tripper was heard one day to say to her friend, 'This is where Sir Betjeman Britten is buried.' Beyond the tamarisk hedge and the storm-worn lychgate lies the sand dune bunkered and deviously routed golf course of St. Enodoc where JB regularly failed, as many do, to get within spitting distance of par, and which inspired him to write one of the best ever, most quoted golf poems

Seaside Golf. The 10th green is but a wayward ball's bounce away from his grave, and the sea that he gazed on and swam in as a child is but a couple or so good drives beyond looming Bray Hill.

His eventual seaside retreat 'Treen' is in the lane coming down from Trebetherick to Daymer Bay adjacent to the family home 'Underwood' that his father built. The cliff tops between Daymer and Polzeath, known as Greenaway, have been spoilt to some extent by the extensive building of too many and too conspicuous seaside homes, and it was so even in his boyhood days; much of the despoiling, to his chagrin, actually promoted by his own family. The view of the Camel Estuary and the Atlantic beyond is accessible to the motoring public by way of a large car park which is now a tyre-worn desert with a seedy oasis of a fish and chip, soup in the basket sort of eatery that attracts middle and lower class alike. It is a sad but incontrovertible fact that if you write enticingly about places as Betjeman did then you can only blame yourself if people want to come and see them. And the Cornish authorities do not seem to be greatly concerned with the look of the place as long as the spenders come.

His first visits to Cornwall were at an age too young for clear remembrance. In

BELOW The attractive harbour of Port Isaac, a favourite Cornish haunt of Betjeman.

THE MAN

the early years they would stay at a boarding-house called 'The Haven'. In 1932 his father built himself the very substantial and stylish holiday home 'Undertown' in a track just off the road to Daymer Bay. When John eventually inherited the house he was able to spend his share of the sales on the small and more modest home almost opposite in the same side lane. Throughout his life he came here whenever he could possibly get away from London and his incessant labours. He spent his last months at 'Treen' and was buried, as he always wished to be, at St. Enodoc.

As a boy he did what most children do on holiday: relishing the sand and sea, joining picnic parties and games with other children, but, especially, as he grew older, preferring to cycle off on his own to the small surrounding villages and their churches – such as the magically interiored church of

St. Protus and St. Hyacinth in Blisland on the edge of Bodmin Moor which he described as 'the first really beautiful work of man that my boyhood remembers' and, as he wrote later in *First and Last Loves* (1952) is 'a living church whose beauty makes you gasp.' It had been lavishly restored by Sir Ninian Comper (one of the architectural names that Betjeman made familiar to the public) with a glitter of gold that lightens the dark interior in an unexpectedly theatrical manner. As he wrote, in a more generalised way, on church restoration:

'Of marble brown and veiné
He did the pulpit make;
He ordered windows stainéd
Light red and crimson lake.
Sing on, with hymns uproarious,
Ye humble and aloof,
Look up! and oh how glorious
He has restored the roof!'

He discovered more Comper in the church of Little Petherick up the other side of the Camel estuary from Wadebridge. He discovered the large, curiously isolated, clean and simple stones of St. Endellion on the road to Delabole and Port Isaac, its small decorative spires making it look like 'a hare crouching in the grass.' And the macabre church of Morwenstowe on the borders of Devon with its vicarage chimneys like miniature

churches, the gothic fancies of its famous vicar, Robert Stephen Hawker whose measured verses inspired him. And always the tiny church of St. Enodoc, dug out of the sand dunes in 1863 where it had been half-buried for many years; where the family went willingly to its services. There his mother is buried and a plaque for his father was later erected. The church is finely commemorated in the poem 'Sunday Afternoon Service in St. Enodoc, Cornwall'. And he found a friendly guide to his burgeoning hobby of churches and his youthful literary ambitions in the bearded rector of St. Ervan on the other side of the estuary beyond Padstow. He introduced John to a strange book called *The Secret Glory* by Arthur Machen, a book that affected him more than any other he read in his boyhood days with its affinity of thought and imagery.

But it was not all churches. There was the wide sweep of the Camel estuary with

ABOVE The holiday home 'Undertown' which the poet's father built in the 1930s.

its notorious Doom Bar where they would look each year to see if yet another unfortunate vessel had been wrecked, and the exciting trip over to Padstow on the ferry from Rock, particularly exciting (but mercifully brief) when the large waves rolling in from the Atlantic caught the boat side-on. Padstow itself, now continually crowded with visitors and ruled over by Rick Stein, was then the epitome of a quiet Cornish fishing village – 'St. Ives without the artists.' On their side of the estuary lay Port Isaac, which you come upon suddenly, clinging to the cliff sides where no place seems likely to be before you rounded the corner, and nearby Port Gaverne with its friendly pub; the walks around Greenaway to the surfer-festooned beach at Polzeath with Pentire Head thrusting out into the Atlantic. All this lay then at the end of a romantic steam train journey into Wadebridge where one would then alight at the station before the line from Bodmin

ABOVE The family left Highgate and moved to 53 Church Street, Chelsea in 1917.

was closed. He used to think this was one of the most thrilling train rides in England. The station is now 'The Betjeman Centre' an old people's day centre, the inspiration of Betjeman's local doctor, Gordon Kinsman-Barker, with an evocative room set aside as a small Betjeman museum.

The feelings of a boy like Betjeman returning to the city after a holiday in Cornwall are movingly caught in *Harrow-on-the-Hill* – the feelings of so many who live in less enchanting places and wonder why they put their roots down in Staines or Slough – or even Chelsea – when they could have lived in Port Isaac.

'When a man is tired of London, he is tired of life,' said Samuel Johnson. Betjeman, who clearly loved Cornwall most of all, always kept a fascination for London, writing warmly and pleasantly about its places and people, and he particularly appreciated the City where he documented the amazing number of churches and its strange lonely quietness at a weekend when the business world has departed to West Wittering and Chichester Harbour. Constant memories of the sea-fresh shores of Cornwall allowed him to exist in the petrol fumes and noise of the city. The ever present longing for fields and fresh air, so frequently evoked in the Cornish poems, is felt in many of his London writings. 'A slight sense of country comes as soon as you get off the Victoria Line at Seven Sisters,' was how he started his *Telegraph Weekend* piece about Tottenham in 1973 – 'roads are broader, skies are wider, trees may be seen in back gardens'. Walthamstow, now a grey place, was different in the days when William Morris lived there with 'scattered red roof tiles and big hayricks'. Any place could be excused if there was a smell of may trees around. He often persuades us that London is simply a collection of villages within easy crow-flying distance of Westminster and the City of London. He persuaded us on many occasions that the now non-existent Middlesex was a rural Elysium.

The time came, as it did and still does for so many middle- and upper-class British

ABOVE Betjeman at South Kensington, the setting-off place for many boyhood excursions.

children, especially boys, to be sent away to school. Whether this custom is perpetuated because it is good for the children or good for the parents has never been made clear. To those who always expected to spend their childhood at home, with school just a daily outing, it seems an unbelievably callous and cruel way to treat one's vulnerable offspring. On the other hand, there are many who believe that it is the best way to develop the future leaders of men. Betjeman's first taste of being a boarder came in May 1917 when he was sent to the Dragon School in North Oxford. But that was comparatively all right as he was among friends. The Betjemans had come to know the Lynams on holidays in Cornwall for 'Hum' Lynam who was the senior master at the school and soon to succeed his greatly loved father, 'Skip' Lynam, as headmaster, also had a cottage at Trebetherick. He became a sort of 'uncle' figure and his children Joc and Audrey were John's close friends, and it was he who suggested that John became a pupil at the school most frequently referred to as 'Lynam's'. The Dragon School was a compassionate organisation for schools of

ABOVE An artistic acquaintance at Marlborough was Anthony Blunt (1907-1983), later a controversial public figure.

that time (a haven by comparison with the badly run Junior School at Highgate) and most of its pupils, later girls as well as boys, seem to remember it with fond affection. Betjeman described it 'as one of the happiest places in the world, and it made all subsequent education seem repulsive.' John enjoyed his days there. He was never very fond of or good at organised games, but found plenty of other outlets to occupy his few leisure moments, drawing and writing, and especially bicycle excursions into

Marlborough College where Betjeman experienced some unhappy times between Dragon School days and Oxford University.

the Oxfordshire countryside under the guidance of 'Tortoise' Haynes, a master with a passion for photography and Norman churches; a love that was clearly passed on to a willing pupil. In 1952 JB dedicated his collection of essays *First and Last Loves* to Haynes 'who first opened my eyes to architecture.' The school laid a great emphasis on poetry and the memorising of it. It was a perfect training for a future poet and John won a school prize for recitation. His great friend at the Dragon School was Ronald Wright, the son of a barrister, who shared his enthusiasm for churches and their religious lore, and became a Roman Catholic at the age of twelve. It was while John was away at the Dragon School that his parents decided to move to 53 Church

ABOVE Magdalen College at the gateway to Oxford where Betjeman went in Michaelmas Term, 1925.

Street in Chelsea, much to his annoyance and genuine loss. There was nothing there to replace the adjacent pleasures of Hampstead Heath and his beloved 31 Highgate West Hill and the new house seemed charmless and cramped. The only compensation was that Ronald Wright lived in Chelsea too, and during the holidays the two boys would explore London, mainly by the Underground from Sloane Square, which they came to know intimately, travelling out as far as Metroland. Other times John would go on his own to seek out the bookshops and began to form his fine collection of books on architecture and churches (now housed in the Library of Exeter University). His father actually encouraged this hobby and urged him to buy well. In a copy of *The Churches of London* by George Godwin he wrote, 'To my dear boy in the hope that his appreciation of all that is beautiful will never fade.' Another friend at the school was Hugh Gaitskell, just five months older; a friendship which was to later continue at Oxford University.

The time came when the gentle care of the Dragon had to be exchanged for the rigours of the English public school. In later years Betjeman spoke in admiration of the products of Eton and Harrow, especially Harrow where he professed he would like to have gone, in spite of his distaste for the years he spent at Marlborough, the school chosen as his next scholastic home. Under the rigorous discipline of

Marlborough life, Betjeman was bullied and humiliated, made to speak the school slang, made to study Latin and Greek which he could never appreciate, made to indulge in sports which he hated, spending too much time, 'shivering in exiguous shorts' and all the other unpleasant aspects of a school that pursued the *Tom Brown's Schooldays* traditions. The food, he said, was atrocious. His friend John Edward Bowle, later an art historian described the school as 'the most awful barbarous place.' Yet in this barren background Betjeman maintained enough spirit to get the best out of it. There was some compensation in meeting with friends and peers of similar tastes like Louis MacNeice and Anthony Blunt. In the mellow introduction to the new edition of *Ghastly Good Taste* in 1970 he reveals how much he was helped by individuals from his school and university days. While his favourite subject of architecture was 'hardly mentioned' in the Marlborough

curriculum, he learned much about it and about art on expeditions with 'that good and hospitable man Colonel Christopher Hughes, the art master. He treated us as adults and led us off on sketching expeditions to remote villages.' Not much good at watercolours himself Betjeman admired the work of John Bowle who won the Art Cup in 1924. In the company of Ellis Waterhouse, later a Professor of Fine

Arts, Anthony Blunt, who became Keeper of the Queen's pictures, and Blunt's elder brother Wilfred, he discovered the work of the French Impressionists and particularly the work of Cézanne. Betjeman always sketched throughout his life in an amateurish but recognisably individual sort of way.

Continually active in the writing field, he helped to found *The Heretick* – a mildly subversive publication intended to undermine the official school magazine

The Marlburian – and wrote for it under a number of disguised names. He had some success as an actor – a career which some of his friends thought he should have followed. He did in a way in his radio and television career. A friend, Philip Harding, took him down to his home in Dorset during one vacation and initiated his love for that splendid county and Thomas Hardy. John developed romantic crushes for many good-looking schoolmates but this is what incarceration at a public school does for many. The worst effect, in his father's eyes was an enthusiasm which he developed for the works of Oscar Wilde, leading to a correspondence with Lord Alfred Douglas who later became an acquaintance.

At last, in 1925, he was able to go to Oxford, scraping in as a commoner, with no scholarship to help his father with the bills, by managing to impress the poetry-loving President of Magdalen, Herbert Warren, with his potential as a poet. An Oxbridge education has always been a strangely amorphous activity with no definite guidelines. It is what every person makes of it for themselves. There is, rightly or wrongly, very little official discipline and each student must make his own rules. For those who hope to become academics themselves the passage through Oxbridge is straightforward. They work hard and get a First then carry on working hard for higher things. For others it is the final gloss on the undercoat of a public school education and the way into something important in

BELOW Sir Osbert Lancaster (1908-1986), celebrated cartoonist, was a lasting friend from Oxford days.

the Church, politics or business. As a bonus to the academic side there is glory to be achieved in sport, oratory and drama. But for a few, of whom Betjeman was one, the mainly unimaginative instruction that so many dons offered, the need to swot and pass exams at only a slightly higher level than offered at a good school, are activities for which there is little room in a head full of poems or plays or novels. It is strange how many of our leading writers have proved unsuccessful academics even though, like Betjeman, they went on to become greatly expert and knowledgeable in a field of learning of their own choice. What counts at Oxford is the chance to mingle and talk with one's peers in a chosen field of activity, while a good degree has never been the passport to being a great poet or novelist.

Betjeman enjoyed every moment of Oxford to the full except the moments he had to spend with his tutor who happened to be a man who many now see as an imaginative writer (and who even became the subject of a romantic film) but who John found a pompous bore whom he greatly disliked and was wholeheartedly disliked by in return. There was a hopeless conflict of tastes and style between John Betjeman and C. S. Lewis although they shared literary and religious interests. 'How I wish I could get rid of this insufferable little prig,'

Lewis wrote in his diary with great feeling, while John in return would pen some snide remark about Lewis whenever the opportunity occurred.

Beyond the academic world he was in his element. He spent as little time as possible in Magdalen, a college full of hearties and sportsmen. After one term he stopped eating in college, preferring to dine at 'The George' (St. George's Restaurant at the corner of George Street and Cornmarket), a popular haunt of the aesthetes, Harold Acton then prominent among them, with whom Betjeman liked to mingle. He gradually accumulated a wide circle of friends who would be of practical value in the career to come. These included the artist Osbert Lancaster, future publishers such as John Murray, editors like Cyril Connolly, fellow poets such as W. H. Auden. The bills for high living, good eating and book buying steadily eroded the allowance his father gave him and led to further friction between them, though it must fairly be said that Ernest was, on the whole, remarkably generous and forbearing.

Later Betjeman lodged in St. Aldate's in a handsome room looking out onto Christ Church. He was taken up by the young but already greatly influential Dean of Wadham College, Maurice Bowra – afterwards its Warden and later Vice-Chancellor of the University. To some he might have seemed a churlish man with a wit that suggested he had bought some of Oscar Wilde's discarded epigrams at auction; he was loud-voiced and domineering but he had the

HEDDON COURT.

SUMMER TERM. 1930

School Order.

(Combined place in all subjects.)

1	Goatly i.	31 {	Brazier-Creagh
2	Roughton		Townsend
3	Engleheart	33	Tims
4	Hollom v.	34	Hughes
5	Hollom iv.	35	Vilvandré
6	Smith	36	Healing
7	Hunter i.	37	Soltau
8	Wright	38	Doswell
9	Tucker iv.	39	deHavilland
10	Geddes	40	Goatly ii.
11	Shaw	41	Johnson
12	Pike i.	42	Dizer
13	Dalrymple	43 {	Bewley
14	Glancy		Hawkins
15	Harcourt ii.	45	Gomez
16	Gaster	46	Sale
17	Bryans	47	Trimble
18	Kendall	48	Savory
19	Pybus	49	Bruwin
20	Murrant	50	Noel-Buxton ii.
21	Branfoot	51	Melville
22	Harcourt i.	52	Upton
23	Orr	53	Todd
24	Miller	54	Banes
25	Barrie	55	O'Connor
26	Noel-Buxton i.	56	Hunter ii.
27	Barraclough	57	Pike ii.
28	Rice	58	Williamson
29	Stevenson	abs.	Simons
30	Messum		Holbrook

Boys whose places have been seriously affected by absence during the Term and Examinations are marked (a) and (ε) respectively.

History.

6

Class A. I. Max. 100.
MR. BETJEMAN.

Hunter i.	84
Goatly i.	81
Roughton	79
Smith	69
Geddes	64
Engleheart	63
Shaw	59
Hollom v.	54
Wright	48
Tucker iv.	47
Hollom iv.	43

Class A. II. Max. 900.
MR. GODFREY.

Dalrymple	608
Glancy	513
Pybus	484
Pike i.	472
Harcourt ii.	422
Bryans	397
Gaster	389
Kendall	373
Barrie	364
Murrant	361
Branfoot	291
Orr	254
Harcourt i.	242

Class B. I. Max. 200.
MR. BETJEMAN.

Rice	145
Stevenson	131
Miller	130
Noel-Buxton i.	122
Messum	118
de Havilland	118
Barraclough	111
Doswell	107
Hughes	105
Vilvandré	95
Soltau	95
Townsend	94
Sale	93
Brazier-Creagh	93
Dizer	92
Bewley	90
Healing	74
Tims	62

Class B. II. Max. 600.
MR. GODFREY.

Johnson	371
Gomez	349
Goatly ii.	324
Trimble	321
Hawkins	282
Todd	268
Melville	240
Noel-Buxton ii.	236
Banes	195
Bruwin	189
Savory	182
Upton	179
Williamson	172
Hunter ii.	155
Pike ii.	115
O'Connor	87

foresight to remark that Betjeman had 'a mind of extraordinary originality; there is nobody quite like him.' Betjeman in return said that he owed most of what he learned at Oxford to Bowra. Their friendship was long and lasting and led to other friendships with such as John Sparrow (later the Warden of All Souls) and a regular editor of Betjeman's works, as was Freddie Furneaux, later the Earl of Birkenhead, and literary-minded dons like A. L. Rowse.

One of his undergraduate friends was John Dugdale whose family lived in a strange and splendid country house built in a multi-domed Indian style – Sezincote, near

Moreton-in-Marsh, Gloucestershire. Regular visits here gave Betjeman one of his first tastes of upper class English country-house life, for which he was to develop a strong liking and admiration, and many of his Oxford and future friends were of the blue-blooded variety. As a result some of his detractors have frequently labelled Betjeman a snob. Truer to say that he was ever an opportunist.

Oxford life is a miniature reflection of the real life beyond. It cultivates characters, it encourages eccentrics, it offers an opportunity to become a biggish fish in a little pool. It leads to the obvious truth that it is 'not what you know but who you know that matters.' Betjeman drew everything that could be drawn out of Oxford, a colourful reputation, a circle of influential friends – everything except what his father had sent him there for: a good degree. But it mattered little. The friendships he made were the passport to many of the opportunities that were to come his way and it must always be emphasised that, through constant voluntary study, he accumulated a really in-depth knowledge of architecture, especially church buildings, writing an architectural column in *Cherwell* from the beginning of 1927 and taking every opportunity to visit Oxford and Oxfordshire's historical and religious buildings. He always maintained a

ABOVE A cartoon of the poet by Richard Cole first printed in 1977 at the time of an enjoyable TV series.

THE MAN

devotion to religion that often seemed at odds with his otherwise frivolous nature. He regularly worshipped at St. Peter-le-Baily which he had known from his Dragon School days. He increasingly attended high mass at Pusey House and established a reputation as an Anglo-Catholic devotee.

He ended up with no degree at all having failed to pass a compulsory Divinity paper (of all things from a future ecclesiological expert) and was ignominiously 'rusticated'. True to that brilliant novel *Decline and Fall* written by another of his

Oxford acquaintances, Evelyn Waugh ('I expect you'll be becoming a schoolmaster, sir. That's what most of the gentlemen does, sir, that gets sent down. . .') he followed in the steps of many of Oxford's scholastic failures, with no clear notion of their destiny, to the premises of Gabbitas Thring, scholastic agents. He was turned down by three schools before they found him a post at Thorpe House Preparatory School, Gerrards Cross, Buckinghamshire at a salary of £30 a term. In October 1928 he was allowed to return to Magdalen for a further try at Divinity, failed again and was sent down for good. (Another version of these academic events came to light during the Bodleian exhibition of 2006).

After holidays in Ireland and a very brief and unsuccessful spell as private secretary to an Irish politician, Sir Horace Plunkett, working either at his flat at 105 Mount Street, London or in Crest House, Weybridge, Surrey, he returned once more to the premises of Gabbitas Thring and managed to obtain a post as assistant master (on the strength of subtly exaggerated claims as to his skill at playing and teaching cricket) at Heddon Court in Cockfosters, East Barnet, at twice the salary he had received at Thorpe House. One of his pupils there, David Engleheart (son of the music and French teacher) later described Betjeman as a 'born teacher, enthusing, fascinating and fun, humble and kind and greatly loved and remembered by his pupils.' His lack of ability at cricket was soon sussed out as amusingly recalled in 'The Cricket Master' an appendix to *Summoned by Bells*. He taught Classics, English, Mathematics, History and Science to classes varying between ten and thirty-two and his pupils achieved good results. He survived there for four terms from April 1929 to July 1930, regularly persuaded by his friends that he was wasting his time

BELOW

Field-Marshal Chetwode became a reluctant father-in-law in1933. He had a heroic military career before becoming Commander-in-Chief in India.

DAILY MAIL WAR ALBUM.

2ᴺᴰ BRIGADIER-GENERAL SIR PHILIP CHETWODE.

THE MAN

teaching, with which opinion he heartily agreed.

Through his friendship with the brother of the editor Hubert de Cronin Hastings, aided by a recommendation from Maurice Bowra, he became, from 1 October 1930, assistant editor of *The Architectural Review*. This large, impressive, glossy and influential journal was published from 9 St. Anne's Gate, a posh corner of London, a house where Lord Palmerston once dwelt. It had its own bar in the basement. While Betjeman was certainly well versed in architecture he was not an ideal employee. He often disappeared 'to see people' and, when he *was* at his desk he was, likely as not, scribbling poems; some of which were printed in the magazine alongside many impressive and wide-ranging articles that he wrote. Many of his editorial items were unsigned or written under other names and students of Betjeman are still trying to work out the full extent of his contributions. He enthused about the current Gothic revival and the Arts and Craft Movement; and took every opportunity to spread his

CERTIFIED COPY OF AN ENTRY OF MARRIAGE

Given at the GENERAL REGISTER OFFICE, SOMERSET HOUSE, LONDON

Application Number 34.1184

	Registration District	ED MONTON					
1933 . Marriage solemnized at the Register Office in the District of Edmonton in the County of Middlesex							
(1) No.	(2) Name and surname	(3) Age	(4) Condition	(5) Rank or profession	(6) Residence at the time of marriage	(7) Father's name and surname	(8) Rank or profession of father
155	Twentyninth July 1933	John Betjemann	26 years	Bachelor	Journalist	Heddon Court Cockfosters	Ernest Edward Betjemann	Art Manufacturer
		Penelope Valentine Hester Chetwode	23 years	Spinster	—	56 Hallam Street W.1	Philip Chetwode	Baronet Field Marshal Army Commander in Chief

Married in the Register Office according to the ___ of the ___ by Licence before me

This marriage was solemnized between us.	John Betjemann	in the presence of us,	Isabel Louise Hope	W.M.Miller Registrar
	Penelope Chetwode		H. de C.Hastings	W.Grimaldi Supt.Regr.

CERTIFIED to be a true copy of an entry in the certified copy of a Register of Marriages in the District above mentioned.
Given at the GENERAL REGISTER OFFICE, SOMERSET HOUSE, LONDON, under the Seal of the said Office, the 20th day of March 1961

MA 582555

This certificate is issued in pursuance of section 65 of the Act 12 & 13 Geo. 6, c. 76 (Marriage Act, 1949). Section 65 (3) provides that any certified copy of an entry purporting to be sealed or stamped with the seal of the General Register Office shall be received as evidence of the marriage to which it relates without any further or other proof of the entry, and no certified copy purporting to have been given in the said Office shall be of any effect unless it is sealed or stamped as aforesaid.

CAUTION.—Any person who (1) falsifies any of the particulars on this certificate, or (2) uses a falsified certificate as true, knowing it to be false, is liable to prosecution

circle of acquaintances in the architectural world meeting people he most admired like C. F. A. Voysey, M. H. Baillie Scott and Ninian Comper, all of whom he later wrote about and became lasting friends with. But even the amount of office life that he managed became to seem a bore and, gradually finding himself more in demand as a writer, he left regular employment for the last time in 1933.

While he was with *The Architectural Review* he published his first book of poems *Mount Zion* (1931) and wrote *Ghastly Good Taste* (1933) 'a depressing story of the rise and fall of English Architecture'. In 1934 he was appointed general editor of the Shell Guides, a task he continued to perform from 1934 to 1968 (from 1962 with

John Piper as joint-editor). He wrote the text himself of *Cornwall* (1934) and *Devon* (1936), and wrote *Shropshire* in collaboration with Piper. He also produced for Shell a series of two-minute travel films and numerous promotional pieces.

A regular source of income was now achieved as film critic of the *Evening Standard*, writing a piece for the 'After Dark' section of the paper from 10 February 1934 to 19 August 1935. He had been given the job after the paper's editor, Lord Beaverbrook, had admired a piece he had written for the *Standard* on 'English Peers'. It was an appointment akin to that of war correspondent as taken up by Boot in Evelyn Waugh's *Scoop* (1938) on the strength of having written a nature column for many years. He would not have had any deep knowledge of the film world at the time. At the end of his year and a half stint in the cinemas of London he wrote his

'Good-Bye to Films' on 20 August 1935:

> 'Films were gradually turning me dotty. I used to come out of a Press showing and caress the bricks in the street, grateful that they were three-dimensional. If I saw a thuggish-looking man with his hat pulled down over his face, I expected to be shot in the back. Worse still I was becoming unable to think. Thinking was being done for me on the screen and not very hard thinking, either. . . Paralysis was creeping over me. . . The old, old story seven times a week is more than enough for the most willing ears after a year'.

He was married to Penelope Chetwode in 1933. It was a fluctuating affair both before and during its course. John had met her in 1931 when she was a somewhat awkward debutante. She was, in many ways, his familiar image of the sporty girl with the strong legs he greatly favoured, full figure, straight hair with a pony fringe, a retroussé nose, a sulky mouth and, when needed, a quelling stare. Her favourite phrase was 'right you are' said in a loud and piercing Cockney voice. She was clever and mad about horses. This was never a strong point in her favour with John who always resented her obsession. He once said to a friend who dropped in, 'If we were horses, we'd have had a cup of tea by now.' She was the daughter of

BELOW Betjeman is commemorated in a magnificent window by John Piper unveiled in the local church of All Saints in 1986.

THE MAN

RIGHT 'The Mead' on the fringes of Wantage became the family home in 1951. It had 7 acres of land where Penelope carried on her various livestock enterprises. The house has two aspects, the back being of a rural nature and the front a Victorian gothic addition which Betjeman thought looked like a railway station. They gave it up in 1972.

Field-Marshall (later Baron) Sir Philip Chetwode, a soldier hero, and, at the time of the marriage, Commander-in-Chief of the Army in India, and her mother was a formidable highborn lady. It was strange that John pursued this marriage, particularly as Penelope's parents were understandably dead against it. They never got over the fact that she had aimed so low in society as to take a poet as a partner. The only point in favour was that they had a number of common acquaintances. At the time all that mattered was that they were madly in love with each other, Penelope especially with John. He did everything he could to irritate her parents, the final annoyance being when they went off and got married in Edmonton Register Office on 29 July 1933 without letting the Chetwodes know. Mr. & Mrs. Ernest Betjemann were in attendance and the ceremony was followed by a select lunch of roast beef and Yorkshire pudding in the Great Eastern Hotel near Liverpool Street station, John's favourite hotel. The marriage was 'blessed' in St. Anselm's, Davies Street. They had a short honeymoon in an Essex inn and then Penelope went back to live with her parents but neglected to tell them about the wedding until September when they were about to return to India. Naturally, this did not go down at all well, and the relationship between the Chetwodes and John remained pretty cool. On one occasion when they met there was a short discussion on how John should address his father-in-law who thought that perhaps 'Sir' was too formal and 'Philip' too familiar. 'Perhaps you'd better call me 'Field-Marshall!'

The newlyweds then 'settled' into married life, living briefly in a sordid flat in Museum Street on John's £300 a year from *The Architectural Review*. There was still no marriage settlement from the Chetwodes. They then moved to an even worse flat in Grove End Road. The generally irregular pattern of things was to be marked by Penelope going off to Germany for three months.

Eventually they ended up in a rented farmhouse, 'Garrard's Farm' in Uffington, Berkshire (now Oxfordshire) in the Vale of the White Horse. The rent was £36 a year. Here their son Paul was born in 1937. Nearby in Faringdon lived the eccentric Lord Berners who became a close friend and notably entertained Penelope's white Arab horse for tea in his drawing-room. They rented Garrard's Farm until 1944 but for some time lived in Ireland when John was posted to Dublin as press attaché to

the Ambassador Sir John Maffey. There they mainly lived in a Georgian mansion called 'Collinstown' near Dublin airport where their daughter Candida was born in 1942. From time to time the British Press has fancifully attempted to prove that Betjeman was working as a British spy. It seems unlikely that this was anything more than passing on a bit of information every now and then, which anyone working in an embassy might be expected to do. Happily for us, an enemy agent detailed to

ABOVE 'Treen' in Trebetherick, North Cornwall was Betjeman's holiday home and where he spent his last days.

shoot John, decided, after reading some of his poems, that any one who wrote like that couldn't possibly be a real spy or any serious danger and gave up the pursuit.

In 1943 they returned to Garrard's Farm and John worked in London for the Ministry of Information. It was during this period while operating from Senate House, London University that he came into contact with the 'sporty and tennis-playing' Joan Hunter Dunn who was assistant-manager of the canteen there. In 1945 they left the Farm and took up residence in the large, rambling, cold and damp former Rectory in Farnborough, near Wantage in Oxfordshire, which was given to them as a belated wedding present by Lord Chetwode. It had no running water, no electricity and had 12 acres of grounds to be maintained. Farnborough now commemorates its most distinguished resident in the local church by a magnificent stained-glass window designed by John Piper which was placed there in 1986. After ten years of this inconvenient mode of existence they achieved a degree of comfort and civilisation by taking up residence in a Victorian house called 'The Mead' on the fringes of Wantage. By now the waywardness of their marriage began to become more obvious. Penelope ran The Mead Waterfowl Farm and a tea-shop in Wantage specialising in homemade cakes known as King Alfred's

ABOVE Betjeman's daughter, Candida Lycett Green, author and journalist, at The Cheltenham Literary festival in 2002. *Photo: Ann Heald.*

Kitchen – nominally in partnership with John whose disastrous presence in the shop was never welcomed. When not tending the children, the goats, the horse and the poultry, she increasingly ran her own career as a traveller and author in India and the East, while John in 1955 took a flat at 43 Cloth Fair near Smithfield Market and St. Bartholomew's where he worked during the week, returning to The Mead most weekends to spend an increasingly torrid time with his horse-loving wife. One foreign au-pair during her period with them thought for some time that John's name was 'Shut-up,' so often did she hear him addressed in this manner. Shared friends and endless visitors kept them busy but their marriage gradually lost its viability and the

ABOVE Betjeman
with his regular
publisher 'Jock'
Murray (1909-1993),
a friend from Oxford
days.

visits to The Mead became less frequent. They always remained friends and never officially divorced even when John found a lasting lady friend greatly to his liking in Elizabeth Cavendish, sister of the Duke of Devonshire. In 1972 it was mutually agreed to sell The Mead which Penelope did at a modest price to a Tibetan family whom she thought would appreciate and look after the place. They sold it quite soon after at a considerable profit.

In 1973 Betjeman decided to leave Cloth Fair, the main reason he gave being the increasingly unbearable noise that persisted throughout the night from his neighbouring workers at Smithfield Market as they unloaded the carcasses of meat. The truth was that he wished to be nearer Lady Elizabeth Cavendish who had, by now, bought a house for him at 29 Radnor Walk off the King's Road in Chelsea, close to her own residence at No. 19 where he would increasingly spend his nights after the day's work at No. 29 helped by his then secretary Mrs. Mountain. From 1971 the onset of Parkinson's disease meant that he needed more attention and Lady Elizabeth increasingly took on the role

of nurse. Penelope took herself off to a house near Hay-on-Wye and John wrote to say that she was not to worry about him as everything was all right. He was now able to continue to enjoy his twenty-year-old affair with Lady Elizabeth but never really found his years at Chelsea exactly to his liking and spent a lot of time in Cornwall. The streets were noisy and dirty and full of dog mess. There was a particularly noisy pub on the corner of Radnor Walk and King's Road, while most of the restaurants were not of the ilk that he fancied, like Rules in Maiden Lane. On the credit side a number of old friends were living nearby in Chelsea: Lord David Cecil, Osbert Lancaster (now married to Anne Scott-James), Cecil Beaton and many others. The move to Radnor Walk clarified the situation with regard to Penelope and Elizabeth and the press, as typified by the *Daily Express* headline of 21 August 1974, 'Old friend Lady Elizabeth comforts Betjeman,' made the most of the situation. Penelope once summed up her part in his life by saying 'You might have called it a stormy marriage, but fundamentally John and I were terribly fond of one another.' Somewhat irritated

The man who made words sing

As Radio 3 assesses the poetry of Sir John Betjeman, who died a year ago, fellow poet Gavin Ewart considers the Laureate's achievement

18-24 MAY 1985

The Teddy Bear and the Critics
Saturday
7.0 Radio 3

I FIRST READ the poetry of John Betjeman in 1938, when I bought *Continual Dew*. This included 15 poems from *Mount Zion* (1932), the first book of all, and was described on the title page as 'A Little Book of Bourgeois Verse', dedicated to that talented aristocratic practical joker, Lord Berners. The blurb, with its tongue in its cheek, said: 'Mr Betjeman has always been a *vieux jeu* verse writer. A well-known left-wing poet has described his poems as "full of the prejudices of the 19th-century bourgeoisie in their most corrupt and inverted forms".'

This was very different stuff from the Eliot and Auden that changed my life in 1932. It was 'camp', it was extremely funny ('Our padre'), a little hard-hearted ('The arrest of Oscar Wilde at the Cadogan Hotel'), but already it had some of the pathos that was later to be one of the hallmarks of his verse ('Death in Leamington' and 'Love in a Valley') and a kind of macabre jollity ('Exeter'). 'Slough', the famous invocation to the bombers of the coming war, is the only poem in the whole of his work that does more than hint that all is not well with England:

And get that man with double chin
Who'll always cheat and always win,
Who washes his repulsive skin
        In women's tears:

And smash his desk of polished oak
And smash his hands so used to stroke
And stop his boring dirty joke
        And make him yell.

But spare the bald young clerks who add
The profits of the stinking cad;
It's not their fault that they are mad,
        They've tasted Hell.

This is the 'unacceptable' capitalist. The poem is very like Auden's satirical poems of that time. Unusually, it has none of the self-conscious 'amusing' archaism of the joke poems - 'When someone different was I', 'the lone conventicle', 'mid the stands and chairs' and so on.

All these poems, with the exception of one or two 'free' ones, have almost identifiable tunes Betjeman is very much a singing poet, with a strong sense of rhythm. Many of these, I imagine, were party pieces

by a press statement that they had been separated for some 30 years, she put the record straight in 1983 by pointing out that,

'We only parted company in 1974 when Sir John settled in London where he is cared for by his long-standing friend Lady Elizabeth Cavendish. I want to make it quite clear that I stayed at home while my two children were growing up. I knew that John, like all poets, had other ladies in his life. I did not mind a bit. I travelled abroad just twice during that time, once to Spain and the other time to India. But I did not really start my travels until my children were grown up. They had no idea about John's relationship with Lady Elizabeth. Indeed my daughter Candida had been married several years before she knew. I knew all along. I did not mind very much. We have always been on good terms. We really separated when he came to London in 1974 to be near doctors so that he could get treatment for his Parkinson's disease. He was already moving rather slowly then. For all that, I am fed up with the impression that we have been separated much longer.'

From that time Penelope contentedly lived her own life, with occasional trips abroad, riding her pony from Cusop into Hay and her notepaper proclaiming gleefully 'No telephone, thank God.' John made very rare visits.

From the earliest days Betjeman had a great gift for friendship and few of those with whom he developed close bonds were ever spurned or forgotten. In 1979 he had drawn up a final will with its usual application to the family. In November, in spite of his ailments, he was still thinking of all those who had meant much to him and in a letter of intent sent to Candida, he asked that all his godchildren (which were many) and his best friends (even more) should be given some suitable item from his house. Twelve godchildren were listed. The list of his friends to be remembered was a reflection of alliances made throughout his life. It included his three literary executors, and close friends such as Jock Murray, Osbert Lancaster, Jonathan Stedall, Joan Kunzer, John Arlott, Ashley Barker, Susan Alison, Kingsley Amis, Dr. Frank Tait, Nancy Willis, Mervyn Stockwood, Harry Williams, Harry Jarvis, Gerard Irvine, John Piper, Adrian Sharpe, Lionel Perry, James Lees-Milne, John Walsham, John Brandon-Jones, Benjamin Bonas, Eleanor Countess of Wicklow, Janet Stone, Sophia Paget, Mrs. Alford and A. L. Rowse.

His last years were increasingly inactive owing to a series of afflictions that added to the burden of his steadily worsening Parkinson's disease. He suffered a stroke in 1981 and a further heart attack in 1983 which resulted in a substantial loss of speech. His old friend Prebendary Gerard Irvine called in regularly to give him communion. On one occasion, breaking long silences, Betjeman suddenly uttered what Gerard Irvine thinks might well have been the last lines of poetry he conceived:
'Of all the things within this house that are by me possessed

WESTMINSTER ABBEY

SERVICE OF THANKSGIVING
for the Life and Work of

SIR JOHN BETJEMAN
CBE

1906—1984

POET LAUREATE

St Peter's Day

Friday 29 June 1984
11.30 a.m.

ABOVE Order of Service at Westminster Abbey 29 June 1984.

LEFT Betjeman became the best-known and most-loved literary figure.

ABOVE For a while, after the burial, a simple cross marked the grave. This is now in the John Betjeman Centre in Wadebridge.

I love, oh yes, I love by far, my *ironing* board the best.'

In May 1984 he was taken, along with Elizabeth and his attendant nurses, to his home in Trebetherick. He was visited there by Candida who found him in serene mood and she read him some of Evelyn Waugh's *The Ordeal of Gilbert Pinfold*. There was some talk of taking him back to London by ambulance on the 18th but he clearly wished to end his days at 'Treen'. He died peacefully at 8 a.m. on 19 May

1984. He would have been amazed and gratified at the amount of media attention his passing attracted.

His funeral was held at St. Enodoc on a dramatic day in August when the heavens opened, the wind and rain drove in horizontally and the graveyard was a sea of umbrellas – a scene unforgettably caught by local artist Joan Cockett who lived near 'Treen'. Very few could squeeze into the tiny church where all was damp and dark and hardly anything could be heard for the noise of the gale outside.

'English weather for a most English poet' said *The Daily Telegraph*.

The press chorus of acclaim for his life and career was even greater than the one that heralded the laureateship:

'John Betjeman, the people's poet, dies aged 77' – *Sunday Express*.

'Frightfully good old Betjeman' said Kingsley Amis in *The Observer*.

'Not since Tennyson has a poet won such renown'

– Philip Larkin in *The Daily Telegraph*.

'Sir John Betjeman: poet and missionary for our cultural heritage' and 'True Laureate' intoned *The Times*.

A few days later there was similar wide coverage for the funeral.

A Memorial Service at Westminster Abbey on 29 June was a suitably joyful occasion as a congregation of 2,000 remembered both the man and his poetry. Prince Charles read from *Ecclesiastes* – 'Let us now praise famous men' and the address was given by an old friend the Rev. Harry Williams who quoted from *In a Bath Teashop*. Perhaps, he said, JB was so loved by so many because he fondly regarded everyone as though they were all potentially 'little lower than angels'. Poems were read by *The Daily Telegraph* racing columnist Lord Oaksey (*Trebetherick*) and Prunella Scales (*South London Sketch*). Princess Margaret and the Duke of Gloucester were there and poets Philip Larkin, Roy Fuller and Kingsley Amis, also Miss Joan Hunter Dunn safely cloaked in the anonymity of her married name. The Order of Service sheet listed the first two items of music played as 'Chanson De Matin' by Ketelbey and 'In a Monastery Garden by Elgar' – but they came out as intended under the direction of his musical collaborator Jim Parker.

The Poet

'I knew as soon as I could read and write that I must be a poet.'

One day on a rare outing with his father they stood together in front of a picture called *The Hopeless Dawn* and Ernest urged him to 'translate the picture into verse.' He kindly gave him some opening lines:

'Through the humble cottage window
  Streams the early dawn.'

Father Betjemann was quite encouraging with regard to poetry in the early days. 'And how's our budding bard? Let what you write be funny, John, and be original.' But he cooled off in his support when he realised that John really meant to be a writer and had no desire to work for the family firm.

If a little early inspiration came from his father, most of it came from the lightly tripping lines, to be found in turn of the century anthologies, by such poets as William Allingham and Thomas Hood. He grew naturally to be a rhyming man, staunchly declaring that he found having to rhyme a source of inspiration – clearly true when you think of *The Subaltern's Love-song*. It was fortunate that her name was Hunter Dunn and not Chrichton-Stuart. And what might have been the result if he had first turned a jaundiced gaze, as well he might, on Staines or Brixton (you couldn't really have Brixton for a rhyme), before Slough came to mind. So if he was poet born to rhyme, the undoubted originality had to come from the use of words and images and the aptness of the poetical connection. Perhaps more of this, than some critics tend to think, came from his contemporaries as well as the past.

Certainly Hardy and Eliot were deeply influential.

Although his earliest verses, as is the general tendency for such things, were traditionally unremarkable, we can perhaps, in hindsight, see a touch of the future Betjeman in a short effort published in *The Draconian*, the Dragon School magazine:

'Hum and May went out one day
On a motor-bike painted vermillion;
Hum was the nut of the latest cut
And May was the girl on the pillion'.

The first wholly unmistakable Betjemanian poem was published in *The Isis* (the leading Oxford undergraduate magazine) in 1928. Entitled *To the Blessed St. Aubin*

it was later re-titled *Hymn* and found its clear inspiration by being a parody of the hymn *The Church's One Foundation*. Early Betjeman poems are either light satires or have a slightly satirical touch. Betjeman came to deplore the label 'satirist' and hotly denied being one; rounding on the blurb-writers and critics who labelled him thus. Nonetheless a strain of satire was there in the beginning though later it became something more personal – perhaps simply a facility for acute observation that gave things a biting edge. Neither was he ever a pure and simple humorist as his appearance in many anthologies of comic verse might indicate. He was, true to his father's wish, a writer to whom being funny was a natural pose and laughter a tonic. The next much anthologised effort was printed, just after he had left Oxford, in the 'other' magazine *Cherwell*. *A Varsity Students' Rag* was one of a handful of exaggeratedly popular poems which he would quite like to have disowned simply because they insistently promoted the lightness of his reputation – an estimation which was to take many years to remove. He certainly can be a very good 'light' poet – not an easy task to be light and lasting in any art – nor is it anything to be ashamed of, now we have overcome the deference to the stuffy Victorian ethos of art that overlaid British culture for so long. We know him now as he would like to be known – as a substantial poet of lasting quality.

1930 saw his reputation further enhanced by such items as *Westgate-on-Sea* published in *The Architectural Review*, his first journalistic employer, and one of his first lasting classics *Death in Leamington* which was to stand out in his first collection of poems, alongside *Croydon*, as true blue Betjeman. The most collectable of his pieces written so far were published in an unusual slim volume called *Mount Zion* or *In Touch with the Infinite* in 1931. This came about through the championship and generosity of a rich dilettante Edward James, a fellow student at Oxford, who

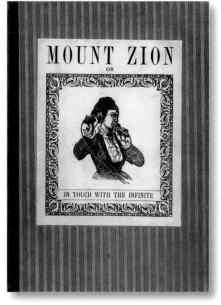

LEFT The fatherly features that were to become well-known on the TV screen.

BELOW *Mount Zion* (1931) was his first book of poems, published by his Oxford friend Edward James (1907-1984).

THE POET

BELOW West Dean in Sussex, the home of the affluent promoter of art, Edward James.

lived in arty affluence at West Dean in Sussex. He was persuaded to publish the poems at his own St. James Press by another pal and admirer of Betjeman, Randolph Churchill. The tongue in cheek kind of production they gave it might have looked like a joke at the expense of the Victorian art that Betjeman already greatly admired without yet having the position and courage to promote it against the fashionable

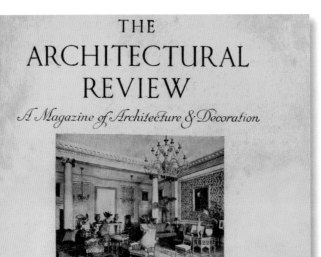

THE

ARCHITECTURAL
REVIEW

A Magazine of Architecture & Decoration

NUMBER 10 DOWNING STREET IN 1904

Incorporating
THE
CRAFTSMANSHIP
SUPPLEMENT

Two Shillings and Sixpence Net.

9 Queen Anne's Gate. Westminster. S.W.1.

Vol. LXXI   March 1932   No. 424

LEFT *The Architectural Review* was his first journalistic home and published many of his early poems.

whims of the day. Printed on thick green and pink paper it was bound with firework-paper leftovers. This insubstantial wrapping meant that, in time, the spines inevitably split so that a perfect copy is now a true rarity. They used stock printers' decorations and Victorian engravings intermingled with six odd little drawings by Hugh de Cronin Hastings, expressing 'the beauty of suburbia'. It was given an encouraging

SEZINCOTE — MORETON-IN-MARSH

CONSTANTLY
UNDER THOSE MINARETS
I have been raised from the deepest depression
and spent the happiest days
of my life.

MRS. ARTHUR DUGDALE

therefore, the hostess of Sezincote, I run risk
of **alienating**
by dedicating to her this precious,
hyper-sophisticated book.

ABOVE *Mount Zion* bore a glowing tribute to Sezincote and its owners.

notice in *The Architectural Review* (December 1931) by (surprise!) Randolph Churchill under the heading *Arts and Crafts*: 'If you like the genuine sublimation of the ridiculous you should read these poems.

All the ugliness of the suburbs, all the vulgarity of human nature, are translated into golden beauty when touched upon by Mr. Betjeman's pen. The book contains some of the wittiest satires that have been produced for some time. The very beautifying of the grotesque in life and architecture with which these poems are principally concerned, brings a heightened sense of the ridiculous.

In the opening poem in the book this young author has achieved very nearly the impossible. His picture of an old woman dying in an upstairs bedroom in Leamington Spa is at once beautiful, poignant, fantastic and absurd.'

The book neither set the world alight nor aroused much hostility. The main person to be upset by it was his father who complained that in the dedication John glowingly mentioned the stately home of Sezincote where 'he had spent the happiest days of his life.' He felt that ought to be moderated a bit to '<u>some</u> of the happiest days'. The other person not wholly pleased at the time was Edward James who complained that Betjeman gave so many copies of the book away that there were none left for him to sell. He may have felt rewarded by his prophetic investment in hindsight and was no doubt grateful for a 'funny and touching tribute in verse' that Betjeman published in *Punch* in October 1958:

'The sun that shines on Edward James
Shines also down on me:
It's strange that two such simple names
Should spell such mystery.'

Edward James clearly and justifiably expected that Betjeman would give him the chance to publish his next book of verse with perhaps a chance to recoup the loss on the first. He was therefore rather hurt to find that Betjeman had agreed to place his work with another old university pal, John Murray, the inheritor of one of London's great family publishing houses who was eager to take Betjeman under his wing. It now seems clear that *Mount Zion* had made more impression on the discerning than was obvious at first and several publishers had the wit to see the dawning new talent therein – including T. S. Eliot who would have liked to add a reprint of it to the Faber & Faber list. But Murray got in first and fell in with Betjeman's idea of reprinting most of *Mount Zion* and adding all the worthwhile things he had written since. Betjeman had a rather fraught meeting with James who eventually, as JB reported 'gave in to me and cleared my conscience for me in the most charming manner' – even though they had been setting some of the new poems in galley form and working on the book-selling fraternity. JB got his poems back, feeling 'a frightful shit', for a modest compensation of £9 which he felt he ought to pay out of any advance that Murray gave him.

There had been no actual agreement with the James Press so Murray was able to settle matters amicably and at the beginning of 1937 ideas for the production of

SLOUGH
IN THE 1990's

A Poetry Competition for Schools based
on Betjeman's view of the town
in the 1930's

Sir Nigel Mobbs D.L.
on behalf of Slough Estates plc and The Betjeman Society
has pleasure in inviting

Mr & Mrs Peter Gammond

to the Prizegiving and Reception
for the Slough Schools Poetry Competition
'Slough in the 1990's'

to be held at
260 Bath Road, Slough
at 6.30 pm on 30th June, 1993

R.S.V.P.
using enclosed card
(Map on the reverse)

SLOUGH
ESTATES

ABOVE Slough never forgave the early poem of that name and has been trying to reverse the impression given ever since.

ABOVE *Continual Dew* (1937) was the first book of poems to be published by John Murray.

the new book were being tossed around. It seems to have been assumed, right from the start, that this would be in the same fanciful vein as *Mount Zion* and Betjeman became involved in endless wrangles over paper and typefaces – matters that always intrigued him – very much a reflection of his architectural interests. The letters passed to and fro in typical abundance. 'I enclose a new poem on Slough' he wrote in February, and was conciliatory about possibly removing the adjective 'stinking'. *Slough* was to become another of the poems that he wished he hadn't written but at the time it was obviously well set for bringing in a bit of media publicity. In typical fashion he lost his publisher's contracts and then found them again. A Victorian print of a 'dripping' tap was considered for incorporation in Edward Kauffer's cover design but was relegated to the title page with the drips properly aligned in a sketch by the poet – and so on and on. At last, in October, he was able to write, 'Thank you so much for the book with which I am delighted. Ted's cover is magnificent. Most appealing and a lovely contrast with the black and gold inside. The gilt edges are lovely. So is the grey paper. Loveliest of all is the prayer-book paper' – this had been inserted for a few poems.

Added to the reprinted items from *Mount Zion*, were such future Betjeman classics as *The Arrest of Oscar Wilde at the Cadogan Hotel*, *Distant View of a Provincial*

Town, the notorious *Slough* and *Dorset* a contribution to *The London Mercury* as far back as 1932. Many of the other poems reflected his colourful church and religious interests; most of them were notable for being unlike anything else being written at the time and the reviews were satisfyingly glowing. Evelyn Waugh, writing in the pages of that short-lived periodical *Night and Day* (to which Betjeman was also an occasional contributor) discovered that, 'Mr. Betjeman's poetry is not to be read, but recited – and recited with almost epileptic animation. Only thus can the apostrophic syntax, the black-bottom rhythms, the Delphic climaxes, the panting ineptitude of the transitions be seen in their true values.' Enough to bring anyone with a fund of curiosity dashing to survey its pages.

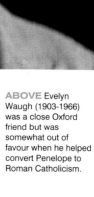

ABOVE Evelyn Waugh (1903-1966) was a close Oxford friend but was somewhat out of favour when he helped convert Penelope to Roman Catholicism.

Betjeman, now full of poetic enthusiasm gently nudged John Murray in 1939 by writing, 'John Miles wants to publish 22 new poems of mine. As you took the risk of publishing *Continual Dew*, I don't want to do anything without first getting your permission.' Murray took the hint and hastened to issue a contract for a new book. They both settled for 'a cheap un-illustrated edition like a Victorian hymn book.' Delighted that Murray was in action again, John engaged in another flurry of ideas

THE POET

RIGHT *Old Lights for New Chancels* (1940), the second book of poems with Murray, bore an anonymous silhouette head by John Piper.

FAR RIGHT *The Listener* was an early publisher of Betjeman's verse, articles [many from radio talks] and reviews.

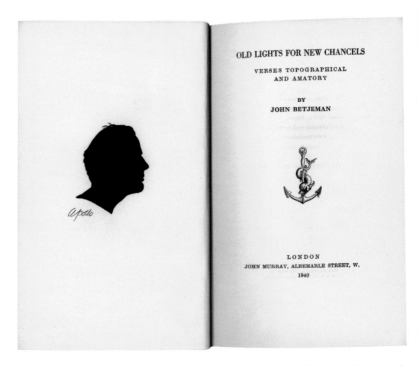

OLD LIGHTS FOR NEW CHANCELS

VERSES TOPOGRAPHICAL
AND AMATORY

BY
JOHN BETJEMAN

LONDON
JOHN MURRAY, ALBEMARLE STREET, W.
1940

about typefaces and other practical points. Meanwhile he was delighted to be courted by Cyril Connolly and Stephen Spender who published *Blackfriars* in *Horizon* and wanted more of his poems for their new magazine – 'Not to be published without John Murray's permission,' he was proud to be able to stipulate. 'How about a silhouette of me' he suggested, and John Piper was asked to provide one with JB's signature beneath but, by request, no credit to be given to the artist. Churchy as ever, the twenty or so titles for the book that he suggested were whittled down to one – *Old Lights for New Chancels* – which he liked but then started to have doubts about – 'a bit of a mouthful isn't it ... how about *The Negligent Incumbent*. As a sub-title *Topographical and Amatory Verse*. But perhaps that should be the main title! Perhaps *Old Lights for New Chancels* is rather nice – although it should be "restored" chancels to be true.'

It is strange to think now that this sombre looking little volume, with no lettering on the spine in church book style, is, in fact Betjeman's book of wartime poetry. But there was no war poetry that you might truthfully categorise as such and it represented most clearly the unruffled middle classes of Britain who went about their lives and jobs with values unaltered. It categorised him once again as a laureate of the people. Just before publication he was concerned that the title was too humorous and cancelled out the serious tone of the preface. 'I hope it is not too late to alter it.' He suggested *A Three Decker Pulpit*. Jock Murray let him ramble on and stuck to *Old Lights for New Chancels* balancing the fact that the Pipers thought it too funny while Osbert Lancaster quite liked it. Betjeman put forward the idea that it would be nice to have a '"Not

THE LISTENER, 22 DECEMBER, 1938. Vol. XX. No. 519. PRICE THREEPENCE

DEBATE ON PRESS FREEDOM

The Listener

Published every Thursday by the British Broadcasting Corporation

Christmas Rush : The Post Office Sees It Through

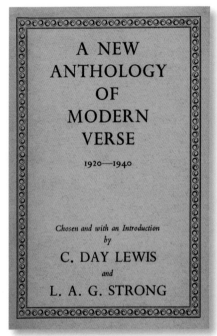

A NEW
ANTHOLOGY
OF
MODERN
VERSE

1920—1940

*Chosen and with an Introduction
by*

C. DAY LEWIS
and
L. A. G. STRONG

ABOVE The poet was delighted to find himself in the pages of innumerable anthologies.

RIGHT The poet W.H.Auden (1907-1973) was an Oxford friend and a lifelong admirer.

recommended by the Book Society" banner wrapped round the cover. That would get the right profile.'

'William Plomer has done me proud in *The Listener*', he joyfully wrote to Murray and indeed the reception of the book was pretty well all that could be desired. Perhaps nobody took much notice of the earnest preface but it has become very much a key to some of his thoughts on the poetry he admired and presumably copied.

'Sometimes the poets I admire never directly hint at their background or age, but they are so saturated in it that they do not have to hint. I find, with this absurd topographical predilection, hardly any pleasure in the Elizabethans, less in the seventeenth century (but this may be due to excessive reverence for those ages from unsympathetic "tutors") and almost the only early poet I can enjoy is CHAUCER. In the eighteenth century, DR.WATTS, SWIFT, ROBERT LLOYD, THOMSON, DYER, SHENSTONE, MICKLE, COWPER and BURNS are easily among my favourites, but for their topographical atmosphere. In the nineteenth century CRABBE, PRAED, HOOD, CLARE, EBENEEZER ELLIOTT, CAPT. KENNISH NEALE, TENNYSON, CHARLES TENNYSON TURNER, CLOUGH, WILLIAM BARNES, MEREDITH, WILLIAM MORRIS and a score or so more. I find great pleasure in what is termed minor poetry, in long epics which never get into anthologies; topographical descriptions in verse published locally at Plymouth, Barnstaple, Ipswich or Northampton, Mullingar, Cork, Dublin, Galway. I prefer the local paper weekly to *The Times* daily.'

It is a rather precious list with some of the obscurer names (Kennish Neale?), perhaps only there for effect.

Within the book there was a perceptible strengthening of the verse, a new polish,

and certainly some of his best writing so far, including a set of five lyrical Irish poems *Sir John Piers* previously privately published in 1938. Pieces of what is now recognised as true Betjemanism like *Upper Lambourne, Pot Pourri from a Surrey Garden, Trebetherick, Myfanwy at Oxford'* and *Myfanwy, Senex* and the wry *In Westminster Abbey* to keep in touch with the comic vein.

He was delighted to find that two of the poems had been included in *A New Anthology of Modern Verse 1920-1940* edited by Cecil Day Lewis and L. A. G. Strong published by Methuen in 1941. But he was also keen to find out from John Murray whether Methuen had sought permission and if they had paid for the right. They had and Betjeman was two guineas better off, and rather pleased. The ability to write poems that would frequently be anthologised was a great help to his career and reputation. The anthology, such as Palgrave's *Golden Treasury,* has always been an important factor in establishing poets and Betjeman had been given his first important push when two of his poems appeared in *The Oxford Book of Light Verse* chosen by W. H. Auden in 1937.

He now regularly sent any new verse he had written to Jock Murray, eager for approval, and by July 1945 he was urging his publishers to bring out another volume of poems aware that he was now in full flow and deeply craved the attention that book form can bring. 'Poems in same binding as *Old Lights,*' he suggested and once more enthusiastically plunged into the intriguing game of finding a suitable title with *Bobs Major*, *Treble Bob*, *A Ring of Twenty*, *Call Changes*, *Ropes and Ringers* – all with churchy leanings and leading by way of *Bats in the Belfry* to the eventual *New Bats in Old Belfries* – after innumerable fresh thoughts on the subject, doubts and ditherings. 'By the way,' he added in a letter to Murray in December, 'do ask your advertising people not to refer to me as a SATIRIST in future. I spent a long time in the last book's preface explaining I wasn't a satirist then; I am even less of one now. What I write may not be poetry to TAMBIMUTTU whoever he may be, but it is certainly not SATIRE.'

It is always fascinating, if fruitless, to speculate on how posterity (in a hundred years or so) will rate Betjeman as a poet. While he may not be up there with Shakespeare or Milton, Tennyson or T. S. Eliot, he will surely have the same lasting value as, let us say,

ABOVE He was a regular contributor to *Punch* during the 1950s – which slightly coloured his reputation.

Thomas Hardy which, by his own reckoning, would be a more than worthy rating. He will perhaps have to overcome the fact that so much of his poetry is built on contemporary references; which it is to be hoped the future commentators will take the trouble to annotate. It is certain that he will have to outlive the incidental indiscretions that led him to write some of the more facile pieces that dilute the high quality of his best output. Perhaps even the fact that so many of his poems appeared in *Punch* may, by association, help to categorise him as a light or humorous writer, as

THE POET

RIGHT Many of his early poems were published in the long-established Murray magazine *The Cornhill*.

JAN. 1944   No. 961

THE
CORNHILL

Contributors include

Max Beerbohm
John Betjeman
Elizabeth Bowen
Maurice Bowra
Osbert Lancaster
Rose Macaulay
Raymond Mortimer
John Piper
Peter Quennell

With illustrations

Two shillings and sixpence

JOHN MURRAY

did many of the anthologies in which he appeared. Whatever the verdict, there is no doubt that much of his reputation will be based on the next two or three published collections with *New Bats in Old Belfries* confirming what the Betjeman idiom was, and *A Few Late Chrysanthemums* (1954) and *High and Low* (1966) confirming and strengthening the impact of his work.

In the pages of *New Bats in Old Belfries* appear a number of Betjeman classics that have really stood the test of time. They are mainly poems rich in topographical and/or sociological associations. They had been regularly appearing in such worthy journals as *Horizon*, *New Statesman*, *The Listener*, *Cornhill Magazine*, if not in the more modernistic outlets guarded by Tambimuttu and John Lehmann. They increasingly include lines and phrases that have taken their place in the literary memory. Pre-eminent among them and, lightly acute, lightly satirical – whatever the poet may have said, more or less the prototype Betjeman poem and by far the most anthologised is 'A Subaltern's Love-song' written in adulation of a Miss Joan

Hunter Dunn, a sturdy, attractive, tennis-playing girl who was the deputy catering manageress of the canteen at London University's Senate House in wartime London when JB frequented the building. 'I bet,' he said to Osbert Lancaster, with his usual perception, 'that she is the daughter of a doctor in Aldershot.' She was. Fortunately for her she got married and thus avoided the notoriety of the Hunter Dunn label.

'And cool the verandah that welcomes us in
To the six-o'clock news and a lime-juice and gin'

BELOW Horsey Mere was a favourite Norfolk holiday site and features in the poem *East Anglian Bathe*.

ABOVE The signs in Wantage point the way to their favourite 20th century resident.

'Into nine-o'clock Camberley, heavy with bells
And mushroomy, pine-woody, evergreen smells'
'We sat in the car park till twenty to one
And now I'm engaged to Miss Joan Hunter Dunn'

are a few of the lines, in a poem unendingly quotable, that come readily to tongue and mind. The more earnest critic may see this as being too glib, too easily parodied, and akin to a music-hall act, but it is, without question, richly memorable.

Backing this came such gems as *Henley-on-Thames* with its evocation of 'beefy ATS / without their hats'; *Parliament Hill Fields* – 'Oh the after tram-ride quiet, when we heard a mile beyond / Silver music from the bandstand, barking dogs by Highgate Pond'; *May-Day Song for North Oxford*– 'Belbroughton Road is bonny, and pinkly bursts the spray'; *In a Bath Teashop* – 'She, such a very ordinary little woman / He, such a thumping crook'; *Youth and Age on Beaulieu River, Hants* – 'Slacks the slim young limbs revealing / Sun-brown arm the tiller feeling'; *East Anglian Bathe* – 'On high the clouds with mighty adumbration / Sailed over us to seaward fast and clear'; and *South London Sketch, 1944* – 'The Nonconformist spirelets / And the Church of

BELOW Henley-on-Thames was the setting for two popular poems.

THE POET

England spires' – and so on. Most of it was anthology tailored.

It was a timely stroke, at this early stage, to issue a volume of *Selected Poems*. Such titles *Selected*, *Collected*, *The Best Of* result in much psychological enhancement of a writer's reputation. A badge of worthiness! Yet another friend made at Oxford was John Sparrow, later the warden of All Souls College, a man of sound reasoning and common sense, who was one of the few, along with Tom Driberg and Jock Murray whose advice John would heed in producing finished versions of his poems. Sparrow took on the job of editing and choosing the contents of the projected volume. In fact the poems more or less chose themselves and there was, at least, no title to dither and wrangle over. The book was plainly produced with a lettered dust jacket and in more or less the same style as the two previous volumes of poetry. Only four items were new to book form: *Indoor Games Near Newbury* – a poem that some rate highly and some find a little A. A. Milne-ish, 'Holds me as I drift to dreamland, safe inside my slumber-wear'; *St. Saviour's, Aberdeen Park, Highbury, London, N* – a poem of new muscularity

THE HARROVIAN

Vol. LXII   No. 23   *March 30th, 1949*

CALENDAR FOR THE WEEK

31 TH 11.30 a.m.   Service in Chapel
       12 noon.   Prize Giving
                   Sports Finals
       5.15 p.m.   Songs

APRIL

1 F Term ends
       The Summer Term begins on Tuesday, May 3, and ends on Monday, July 25.

UP! UP!

Where people run, two overcoats stand intent at the end of the track gazing absorbedly into crystals. Every now and again they give out a sudden, vehement cry just before the runners reach them. To strangers, perhaps, it is merely the earliest sound of spring; but the people who run know only too well that the exclamations are heavy with fate.

Day after day we hear their cry, "Up! Up!" Day after day we try to beat it; day after day we arrive a yard too late. We feel like Tantalus reaching out for a cluster of standards which always elude us just as they seem within reach. Ixions may revolve dismally in the discus circle. Sisyphi may vainly try to put weights several times too heavy for them, but their failures can never be so frustrating as the runner's missing yard. When this frustration happens more often than is tolerable, it becomes unnerving. You dream of mammoth heats in which you are competing against all the giants of old and new. "On your marks"; you get down; "Get set," you put your back up; "Go! . . . Come back!" The procedure is repeated. Your soporific self-confidence is shaken by this false start; "Go!" . . . they're off! record-breakers all of them; but you? Your shoes get stuck in the hole you have made, and you stand rooted to the spot. Then you hear the cry "Up, Up, Up, Up, Aup, Aup, Auf, Auf." You wake in a panic. A dog is barking furiously outside your window and your night's sleep is shattered. And even that is not all. Next door there is a gramophone upon which Charles Trenet, that creamiest of French singers, is scraped out at least three times a day. Of his *libretto* all that can ever be heard is the two unmistakable words—" 'Op, 'Op." This can hardly be coincidental.

To the stranger the running-track appears to be a fun-fair of enjoyment. Everywhere crowds of gay colours ripple in the sun. The parade-ground is a fine vantage-point for spectators and non-spectators alike. Among the latter, every species of dog is represented in the sport and gamboling which goes on there; but we fear that " their blood now runs in idler sons," since the days are gone when that stalwart Sealyham competed in the four-forty to extract cries of " The Grove! The Grove! " This year, canine criticism of human athletic prowess has turned from constructive to destructive, and doggy efforts to transform the "hundred" into an obstacle-race have not been entirely unsuccessful. But even if dogs have retired from competition, at least one ardent fairy cyclist has taken up the challenge and is to be seen regularly training, perhaps—who knows?—for a surprise entry in the Monitors' Bicycle Race.

By the time this appears in print, the fun-fair

to-morrow it will have been. But remember Tantalus, remember your own experiences, in dreams and out of them, and above all remember, that however much you try to come up to standard, there will always be people to tell you "You're not a credit."

HARROW-ON-THE-HILL

After his visit to Harrow to deliver the Yates Thompson Art Lecture a few weeks ago, Mr. John Betjeman composed the following little poem which he has kindly allowed us to print. He describes it as being " some verses about the feelings of a child in Wembley Park when it comes back from a seaside holiday in Cornwall."

When melancholy Autumn comes to Wembley
  And electric trains are lighted after tea,
The poplars by the Stadium are trembly
  With their tap and tap and whispering to me,
        Like the sound of little breakers
        Spreading out along the tide line
        When the estuary's flooded
        By the sea.

Then Harrow-on-the-Hill's a rocky island
  And Harrow churchyard full of sailors' graves
And the constant click and kissing of the trolley-buses
        hissing
  Is the level to the Wealdstone turned to waves.
        And the rumble of the railway
        Is the green Atlantic rollers
        As they gather up for plunging
        Into caves.

A thunder cloud is rising over Kenton,
  There's a line of harbour lights at Perivale,
Is it rounding rough Pentire in a flood of sunset fire
  That little fleet of trawlers under sail?
        Can those ships be only roof-tops
        As they stream along the sky line
        In a race for port in Padstow
        With the Gale?

DEBATING SOCIETY

Rules, we are told, are invented to be broken. Perhaps then there is a certain naïve innocence about the members of a society, domesticated by a long series of unbending chairmen, who can find that delight in a mere suspension of rules which is usually reserved for the breach of them. Yet on Saturday, March 19, the motion "that the speeches from the chairman's right are better than those from his left" was enjoyed as the pretext for a licensed Saturnalia.

G. K. Beattie, *Rendalls*, was kind enough to devote his opening speech to the instruction of his audience in the art of speaking. In this *Debater's Vademecum* he laid down four maxims: clearness of diction, conciseness, relevancy and posture. The third he considered out of place in this debate and, indeed, since the opposition had not yet had the chance to speak, had he been strictly relevant, he could only have claimed that his own oration was best by default. His other points he also disregarded, but no doubt of set purpose that he

with Eliot-like imagery 'With oh such peculiar branching and over-reaching of wire / Trolley-bus standards pick their threads from the London sky'; *Beside the Seaside* – an augur of *Summoned By Bells,* printed at great length in *Strand Magazine* and somewhat shortened for the book, and similarly expansive in blank verse *North Coast*.

Of special noteworthiness is John Sparrow's Preface which did much to define the particular qualities of Betjeman's poetry '…he is not a Nature poet, like Wordsworth, but a landscape poet, like Crabbe. And, like Crabbe, he is a painter of the particular, the recognisable, landscape; his trees are not merely real trees with their roots in the earth, they are conifers with their roots in the red sand of Camberley, "feathery ash in leathery Lambourn," or "forsythia in the Banbury Road." Then, having quoted *Henley-*

on- Thames – 'And red the bright geraniums swing / In baskets hanging down', *Trebetherick* and *A Lincolnshire Tale* he says 'Just as some people are fascinated by human beings, by their diversity and their peculiarities, so he has been fascinated by the peculiarities of various places, enjoying each simply for being what it is' …'This topographical predilection, as he calls it, draws him not only to the country-side, where earlier pastoral poets have sought to indulge it, but to the town and, above all, to the suburbs.' To refuel an enthusiasm for Betjeman, if that should ever be necessary, one need only read this Sparrow Preface to be filled with the urge to get back to the poems once again.

Such enthusiasms had, in fact, just previously been set alight by the publication

LEFT *Harrow-on-the-Hill* appropriately made its first appearance in the Harrow School magazine in 1949.

BELOW Fame, indeed, when your name becomes public property.

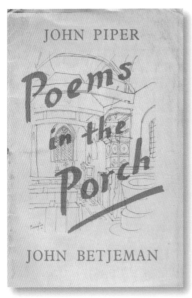

JOHN PIPER

Poems
in the
Porch

JOHN BETJEMAN

in America of a selection of Betjeman's verse and a few pieces of prose from earlier books under the contrived title of *Slick But Not Streamlined* – a title which JB did not like at all but sensibly did not fuss about too much. It was selected and introduced by his old Oxford chum W. H. Auden. His enthusing introduction is as seductive, in its way, as Sparrow's, beginning, 'It is difficult to write seriously about a man one has sung hymns with or judiciously about a poet whose work makes one violently jealous. Normally when I read good poetry, for example Mr. Eliot's line "The place of solitude where three dreams cross", my reaction is one of delighted admiration; a standard of excellence has been set in one way which I must try to live up to in mine; but when I read such lines of Mr. Betjeman as "And that mauve hat three cherries decorate / Next week shall topple from its trembling perch / While wet fields reek like some long empty church", I am, frankly, rather annoyed because they are not by me.' After two such resounding recommendations the impact of the Betjeman touch began to affirm itself.

The next book of poems came as a confirmation of Betjeman's prowess and indeed many critics felt that it outplayed *New Bats in Old Belfries* with a new strength, sureness of touch and depth of feeling in general. Once again the prospects of a new book of poems set Betjeman's mind racing on matters of choice of material and title as indicated in the letter he wrote to John Murray in October 1953, 'As to title, Goldilegz [Myfanwy Piper] thought of A FEW LATE CHRYSANTHEMUMS & I like that very much. The most honest title would be GLOOM, LUST & SELF PITY or we might be purely topographical & call it BAKER STREET & OTHER POEMS' and so on – and (by December) 'I have thought of two good titles for the book. "*Elevenses*" or "*Morning Coffee at Bobby's.*" I think they sum up just where I stand in literature, with Uncle Tom as dinner, de la Mare and Blunden, Spender, Auden and Day Lewis as lunch, the younger poets as

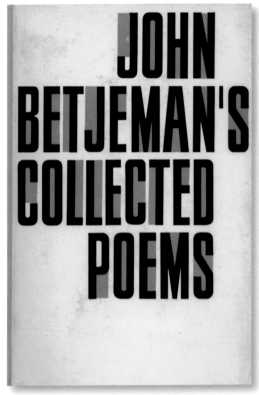

ABOVE The *Collected Poems* as published in the USA in 1958.

breakfast and Andrew Young as tea. Anita prefers "*A Few Late Chrysanthemums*".' And so it stood; although the doubts continued, 'Enclosed are the corrected proofs of my verse, including all the Sparrovian alterations to which we have both agreed. I think it unlikely that the book will have any success, and I should not print more than a few hundred copies ... I dread the reviews!'

The book contained some of his undoubted masterpieces, poems of perfection and intimate effect like *Christmas* which was to be second in ultimate popularity to *A Subaltern's Love-song* and which has become essential Christmas fare without ever losing its impact; *Harrow-on-the-Hill* – 'When melancholy Autumn comes to Wembley / And electric trains are lighted after tea'; *Middlesex* – 'Where a few surviving hedges / Keep alive our lost Elysium – rural Middlesex again'; *Seaside Golf* – 'The very turf rejoiced to see / That quite unprecedented three'; *Norfolk* – 'A whispering and watery Norfolk sound / Telling of all the moonlit reeds around'; *The Metropolitan Railway* – 'Then out and on, through rural Rayner's Lane / To autumn scented Middlesex again'; *'Sun and Fun'* – 'And a host of little spiders / Ran a race across the ciders/ To a box of baby pollies by the beer'; and the deeply moving melancholy of such poems as *Devonshire Street W.1*, *The Cottage Hospital* and *Business Girls*. In this book we are enclosed in the Betjeman world as one perfect poem after another steps forward; not just the *one* memorable item that appears in most books by other poets, but a dozen and more that will not leave the mind.

78   LITTLE BOOK OF **BETJEMAN**

In 1954 a slim paperback was published, with permission, by The Society for the Promotion of Christian Knowledge, a clear acceptance of his standing as a *church* poet, It was given the title *Poems in the Porch* and was illustrated by John Piper. Most of the contents, in fact, were not his best, but one poem made a notable entry into the ranks of ever popular verse – *Diary of a Church Mouse* which has delighted many children as well as adults since its appearance. He could scarcely deny that it was satire, but of so light and genial a touch that it could simply get away with being

LEFT *The Spectator* was a regular outlet for poems and prose including, 1954-1958, a weekly column *City and Suburban*.

graded 'funny'. 'But all the same it's strange to me / How very full the church can be / With people I don't see at all / Except at Harvest Festival.'

A splendid new volume under the title of *Poems in the Porch* was published in 2008 under the editorship of Kevin Gardner containing not just the original six poems but now 22 *Radio Poems* that came from BBC West of England programmes from 1953 to 1957. Nine of them were printed for the first time and the new compilation proved to be a rich and highly entertaining harvest. David Pattison remarked in his review 'they began as mildly satirical and humorous accounts of stages in the Church's year and end as

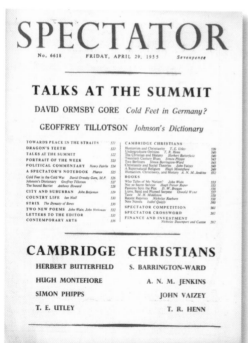

searching and often moving assertations of faith'.

During the period that followed Betjeman became a regular contributor to the much revered or reviled (according to your brow – or class) *Punch*. Founded in 1841 as a strongly radical paper it tended to become blander and less politically biased over the years. It was generally assumed that it was meant to be funny, a description that at certain periods proved somewhat inapt. In the fifties when Betjeman joined the famous table it was going through an imaginative period mainly under the editorship

JI—94

Summoned
: by Bells :

John Betjeman

John Murray Albemarle Street London

SUMMONED
♡ BY BELLS ♡

JOHN BETJEMAN

♡   ♡   ♡   ♡   ♡   ♡   ♡

JOHN MURRAY ALBEMARLE STREET
LONDON   MCMLX

of Malcolm Muggeridge, another Betjeman admirer and friend, who reigned from 1953 to 1957, preceded from 1949 to 1952 by Kenneth Bird (who drew cartoons under the name of 'Fougasse') and succeeded by Bernard Hollowood 1958-1968; covering its funniest and well-loved period before it started to get too clever under succeeding editors and eventually went out of business. It was a pleasing thing to be a *Punch* regular at that time but the character of the paper did rub off on its contributors and it was not surprising that Betjeman's funny and cosily middle class side did tend to overshadow his more powerful assets. Particularly as some of the poems appeared in *Punch* lavishly illustrated by E. H. Shepard, best known for his unforgettable 'Winnie-the-Pooh' drawings. Not too much must be made of this allegiance but it is difficult not to feel that the view of Betjeman that prevailed throughout the fifties was definitely coloured by his being a contributor to *Punch*. The poems that appeared in its pages were in his most urbanely middle to upper

JOHN BETJEMAN

SUMMONED BY BELLS

A Verse Autobiography

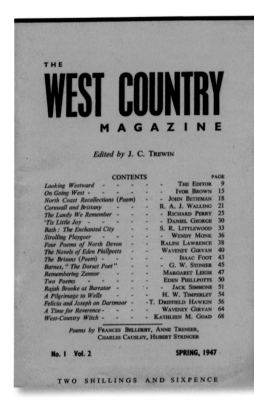

ABOVE Numerous small magazines had JB contributions, The West Country Magazine printing a long poem in 1947.

middle class style. Lasting gems such as *The Metropolitan Railway*, *Seaside Golf*, *Harrow-on-the-Hill*, *Middlesex*, *Greenaway* – contriving to be both polished and poignant. They clearly marked him as the sort of poet unlikely ever to be found in the pages of *Penguin New Writing*.

In 1958, while he was busily occupied producing a weekly contribution to *The Spectator, City and Suburban*, another slim selection appeared in a series of *Pocket Poets* issued by the Hulton Press under the guidance of Rev. Marcus Morris. It was an obvious selection with only one item new to book form 'N.W.5 & N.6' but helped to cement the poet's growing reputation. It was overshadowed, however, by the issue (perhaps premature issue in some respects) of Betjeman's *Collected Poems*. Although the title may well suggest an end to a writing career here it proved to be almost a new beginning. It was a project that delighted and excited the poet, as it clearly should, in spite of all his usual modest qualms. He was greatly concerned, even more than ever before, that all the finer points of publication should be got right.

The title was easy but he clearly wanted, and rightly so, a dignified and aesthetically pleasing production. The decision of what to exclude or abandon caused much thought but JB seemed to have great confidence in his editor, this time, rather unexpectedly, the Earl of Birkenhead, a bookish Oxford friend, generally referred to as *Freddie*. Betjeman was most concerned with the paper and binding. To the art editor Miss Boulanger he wrote, 'Please on no account let any of the designs you sent for wrappers or binding be proceeded with… As regards wrapper (1) the effect is of nothing – of no period & the lettering is out of key with Edwardian typography while the wreaths & device on the back look like somebody imitating an imitation of Rex Whistler ... wrapper (2) the artist has created the effect of a textile design for London Transport (c.1935).' He recruited Osbert Lancaster to help get things

into shape. In the end a tasteful volume generally pleasing to all was produced, with a nicely balanced and discerning Introduction from Freddie, which JB found 'immensely flattering'. The results were beyond everyone's expectations. The first edition of 100,000 sold out in 10 printings, and an even larger edition was needed by 1962. It continues to sell (by now over 2.5 million of the various editions having been purchased), and has since undergone all manner of sea changes. It was expanded in new editions to include subsequent new collections of verse and currently includes all that Murray's consider worth saving; and later editions now including *Summoned By Bells*.

This epic had long been occupying the poet's mind. Perhaps only a poet with Betjeman's particular historical sense and outlook would have been motivated by the idea of following the steps of Wordsworth and producing a verse autobiography, and having the wisdom to put it into blank verse rather than attempting to maintain something in the jingling couplets of Pope or the pounding stanzas of Byron. Not that early autobiographies were anything unusual in the 20th century; they were more or less pouring from the presses but few were cast in blank verse. Betjeman had little optimism

BELOW A delightful collection for the young reader annotated by Irene Slade and illustrated by Edward Ardizzone.

ABOVE He often contributed to local church magazines.

to spare for the idea and referred to his work in progress as something which 'few will read and fewer praise, but which is what I want to do.' He had first sent an early draft of his project to John and Myfanwy Piper as far back as 1941, then always referring to it as *The Epic*. Most of the early chunks were on the subject of Cornwall and his holidays there and a portion of it was published in *West Country Magazine,* under the title 'North Coast Recollections', in 1947. This was reprinted in the *Selected Poems*. Over the years there were unending additions and even more subtractions of passages that he thought might hurt someone, notably his parents or which, in the opinion of the loyal John Sparrow and others whose advice he accepted like Tom Driberg, might even hurt his own reputation. The ins and outs, comings and goings, of *Summoned by Bells* are the meat for a fascinating study which, surprisingly, no-one has yet attempted beyond the excellent chapter in Bevis Hillier's third volume of the biography *The Bonus of Laughter*. Its progress was frequently mentioned to John Murray, who may well have been a little daunted by the idea. In a letter dated 10 February 1960 Betjeman is able to say 'The Epic is finished today but not yet revised & sent down.' There followed the usual furore about titles and binding and wrappers and print until the elegant produced volume of

The Great Work, as it was referred to by John G. Murray, appeared in November 1960 – with Betjeman waiting with crossed fingers and full of fearful doubts. Some of the responses were hurtful and downright spiteful; others hailed it as his greatest achievement. It has now settled into acceptance as a unique masterpiece.

A selection of his work – *A Ring of Bells* – intended for children but suitable for all, was edited by BBC producer Irene Slade in 1962 and delightfully illustrated by Edward Ardizzone. It offered educational guidance by interestingly grouping poems under biographical headings and did nothing but enhance his now tremendous reputation. It is almost predicable, at least on the British arts scene, that peaks of high praise must be followed by phases of debunking. It is in the nature of the British media. From now on there was always going to be some journalistic hack ready to claim that Betjeman was over the hill. On the other hand, the discerning admirers were still avid for more and found an increasing depth and perception in the volumes to come which included *High and Low* in 1966. In it there is not the same percentage of 'hit' poems as was to be found in *New Bats in Old Belfries* twenty years earlier, but there was a body of sensitive and moving poetry, more stark drama too, as if the handbrakes had been taken off. Headed by a rhyming preface:

'MURRAY, you bid my plastic pen
A preface write. Well, here's one then.
Verse seems to me the shortest way
Of saying what one has to say,
A memorable means of dealing
With mood or person, place or feeling.
Anything extra that is given
Is taken as a gift from Heaven.'

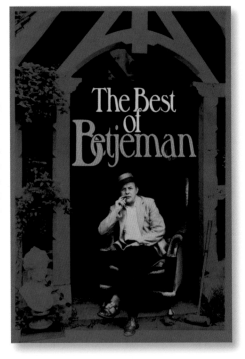

BELOW A discerning choice of poetry and prose edited by John Guest in 1978. 'The Mead' front porch features on the cover in a familiar Douglas Glass photo.

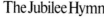

The Jubilee Hymn

Written for the occasion of the Silver Jubilee of Her Majesty the Queen
Words by Sir John Betjeman, Poet Laureate. Music by Malcolm Williamson, Master of the Queen's Music

There followed the delicate scene painting of *Cornish Cliffs*, the shock tactics of *Tregardock* – 'And I on my volcano edge / Exposed to ridicule and hate / Still do not dare to leap the ledge / And smash to pieces on the slate' – and with Cornwall ever the inspiration, the vividness of *By the Ninth Green, St. Enodoc* and *Winter Seascape*.

After a gap of eight years, during which he produced a notable succession of prose works, Betjeman chose a rather chilling title for his next poetry collection *A Nip in the Air* in 1974, but then he had been putting on an act of being aged and decrepit ever since his fifties. He frequently dwelt on death. The opening poem sets the melancholy tone. *On Leaving Wantage 1972* was first published in a local magazine *The Country Churchman* and ended:

'Momently clinging to the things we knew –
Friends, footpaths, hedges, houses, animals –
Till, borne along like twigs and bits of straw,
We disappear below the sliding stream'

This last line was subsequently altered to 'We sink below the sliding stream of time'. There is a sense of the poetry being less spontaneous, more contrived and self-parodying. Some that follow are not among his very best poems – *On a Painting by Julius Olsson R.A.*, *Beaumaris December 21, 1963*, *Hearts Together*, *Aldershot Crematorium* – and so on; perhaps no one poem leaps to life as so many did in *New Bats in Old Belfries*. It was sensible then to refurbish his reputation with one of the many 'selections' that would appear both during his lifetime and after with a ready response from his faithful followers. The ultimate accolade of a Penguin volume called *The Best of Betjeman* came in 1978. Edited by John Guest, it simply chose, chronologically, a selection from each of his volumes of verse, and rounded the book off with seventeen well-chosen pieces of prose including the early 'ghost' story *Lord Mount Prospect*, various topographical pieces, the expertly excellent Introduction to *English Parish Churches* (which had always outweighed the often perfunctory handling of the county-grouped church entries) and items from radio and TV. His prose works, appearing in an amazing assortment of outlets, and considered by the poet as hack journalism, were to become increasingly noticed and valued in his later years and after.

Throughout his active writing career Betjeman had been subjected to the ups and downs of media opinion from a press always eager to find fault. He was extremely sensitive to criticism and always expected the worst of receptions when each new book appeared. Writing was enjoyable when a good poem was brewing but he found having to write to demand, whether it was a weekly article or a laureate poem, an intolerable burden and the deepest of depressions ensued. A notable low point came in 1977 when he had the task of providing verses for the Queen's Silver Jubilee to be set to music by The Master of the Queen's Musick, the Australian composer Malcolm Williamson. Prince Charles had been particularly keen that it should be written, and, although Betjeman was tempted to, in the end he could hardly turn

LEFT & ABOVE
The much-criticised 'Jubilee Hymn' with music by Malcolm Williamson was printed in the Silver Jubilee Souvenir booklet of 1977.

down the royal command. His mind went a total blank and he just couldn't even make a start on the task. Deep despair set in as he contemplated the reception his enforced doggerel would receive. With the help of two friends who lived in a cottage near Penelope he managed to pen the required number of verses and got them off to Prince Charles in time for them to be attached to the equally uninspired music of Williamson. It was revealed in later years that even the Prince was not exactly thrilled by what he had received and had thought of asking Betjeman to try again. But by this time it was too late and things had to go ahead as they were. The *Jubilee Hymn* was first performed in the Albert Hall on 6 February 1977 and, true to form, the Albert Hall audience applauded long and enthusiastically. The dreaded backlash came in the press the next day led by established papers such as *The Times* and *The Guardian*, who gleefully quoted Nicholas Fairbairn, Conservative MP for Kinross and North Perthshire who has said that it was 'absolutely pathetic ... the most banal, ninth-rate piece of child's verse,' and suggested that JB should be sacked. Lady Wilson had read one of her poems at the same event and many thought that she would be a much better candidate for the post. It was staunchly defended by The Master of the Queen's Musick who wrote, in terms of ignorant innocence, that Betjeman had spent a long time over it and had written with great care and love.

'For our Monarch and her people,
United yet and free,
Let the bells from ev'ry steeple
Ring out loud the Jubilee.'

It was, fortunately, an infrequent lapse and JB's publishers in the 1980s, not unexpectedly, started looking for various profitable ways of cashing in on his popularity, and brought out in 1981 a volume

LEFT John Piper (1903-1986) became a close friend after first collaborating on the *Shell Guides*.

BELOW Piper was also the illustrator of the elegant book of *Church Poems* (1981).

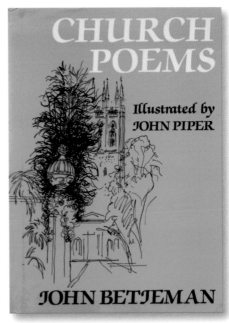

THE POET

of his *Church Poems* beautifully illustrated by his old friend John Piper. Some of the poems were old friends; some had been written and illustrated while Betjeman and Piper had been travelling round the country working on the Shell Guides. John had not been greatly involved in making such a selection and, now declining in health, was having some of the book read to him when the reader ground to a halt when, as the poet well knew, there were more lines to come. 'Well, go on then'. 'But that is all there is'. On discovering that more than one poem had been accidentally truncated Betjeman went berserk. The whole edition, with review copies already sent out, had to be withdrawn and scrapped.

Such is the nature of collecting that, of course, many of the faulty copies were kept and treasured in the same spirit that stamp collectors treasure misprinted stamps. Those that survived are now bartered around at inflated prices. Fortunately the projected limited edition, elegantly printed and signed by Betjeman and Piper, had not yet been issued and was able to go out unsullied. Murray's rather lame excuse for the incident was that the office window had been open and the proofs had been blown out. They made up for their losses by raising the price of the corrected edition by a pound.

Betjeman's indefatigable biographer Bevis Hillier had discovered while researching the Betjeman archive at Victoria University in Canada a number of manuscript poems that had not been published in book form before and most of them not printed anywhere. Under the title of *Uncollected Poems* the book appeared in 1982. The pieces came from all periods of his creative life and covered all aspects of his writing from the comic to the grim. As Betjeman and his friends had chosen to keep them out of

15th September 1976

Dear Mrs. Saunders,

Thank you very much indeed for your kind letter.

Yours gratefully,

John Betjeman

Mrs Lilian Saunders,
2 Rutland Lodge,
Petersham,
Richmond,
Surrey

ABOVE A collection of his Cornish writings sadly coincided with his death there in 1984.

the public eye so far it might be a natural assumption to dismiss them as second-rate scraps purely of rarity interest. Perhaps there is no single poem that one would rate as being amongst his very best. But there were many that have overcome their neglect and are now rated as interesting and enjoyable Betjemania. One of his best purely funny poems is *The Lift Man* originally written for a Gerard Hoffnung Festival Hall entertainment. One of his most introspectively sad is about his beloved bear *Archibald* – 'And if an analyst one day / Of school of Adler, Jung or Freud / Should take this agèd bear away, Then, oh my God, the dreadful void!'

Throughout the years Murray's had adhered to the archaic but pleasing custom of issuing limited, boxed and signed editions for the dedicated and affluent and these have greatly enhanced the pleasure and effort of collecting Betjeman. The first to be so enhanced was *Mount Zion* in a rather indefinite number followed by 29 lavish copies of *Old Lights for New Chancels* (both of these virtually unobtainable nowadays), but the practice was regularised in 1945 with *New Bats in Old Belfries* (1945) – 50 copies, *Selected Poems* (1948) – with a meagre 18 copies, making it one of the rarest of all Betjeman items; *A Few Late Chrysanthemums* (1954) – 50 copies; *Collected Poems* (1958) – 100 copies; *Summoned by Bells* (1960) – 125 copies, and a special 'Jubilee' edition in 1977 – 100 copies; *High and Low* (1966) – 100 copies; *A Nip in the Air* (1974) – 175 copies; *Church Poems* (1981) – 100 copies and *Uncollected Poems* (1982) – 100 copies.

The Betjeman collector has been fortunate in the assorted compilations that have been published since he died in 1984. In that year came *Betjeman's Cornwall*, an enjoyable selection of his West Country writings, 22 items, in paperback only, with an atmospheric photo by television producer Jonathan Stedall on the cover. Just the thing to slip in a pocket or handbook to enliven a visit to North Cornwall. Betjeman's allegiance to Cornwall was second to none and the visitor to the area that he loved can relate the poet to the place (indeed it is difficult not to) more securely than to any other area he wrote about.

With similar intent, but on a more substantial scale, came another paperback collection *Betjeman's London* (1988) its contents chosen by Pennie Denton, a colleague from BBC days. She searched wide and wisely to put together a fascinating poet's-eye view of the city that fascinated him so greatly throughout his life. This also marks the beginning of a deeper and wider interest in Betjeman's prose writings many of them lost to the general public, buried in the past issues of newspapers and such periodicals as *Time and Tide*, *The Listener*, *The Spectator* – the pieces contributed to this last under the ongoing title of 'City and Suburban' revealing a valuable haul of gems among the practical week-by-week journalism.

With such a valuable property at their disposal it is hardly surprising that the publishing house of John Murray has issued a number of attractively illustrated editions of his poems beginning with *The Illustrated Summoned by Bells* (1985) which was greatly enhanced by the drawings of Sir Hugh Casson, a close colleague and

ABOVE An even wider collection of London writings, edited by Pennie Denton, followed in 1988.

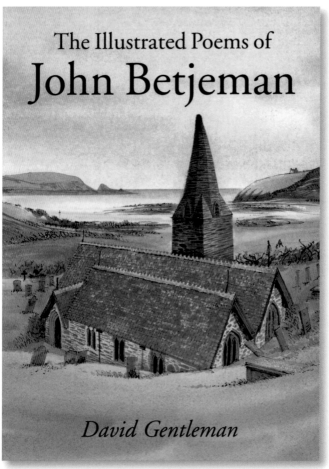

The Illustrated Poems of

John Betjeman

David Gentleman

friend of Betjeman who casually caught the spirit of the poem to perfection. This was followed in 1995 with *The Illustrated Poems of John Betjeman*. The artist chosen for this was David Gentleman, well-known for his many designs for British pictorial stamps, a lively artist with a popular middle class sort of style who came up with some delightful items mingled with some that might well be considered a little twee, emphasising a side of Betjeman that some of his more serious appreciators find a little embarrassing at times.

In 1996 came *In Praise of Churches* a considerable prose and poetry enlargement of the field earlier covered by *Church Poems*. The artist chosen was Paul Hogarth who also caught the Betjeman spirit to perfection giving a poetically coun- trified, rather than holy gloss to the poetry. Three volumes certainly to be savoured by an- yone who enjoys tasteful book production as well as poetry.

There are not many poets in the 20th century who have been so handsomely displayed.

The tradition was continued when The Folio Society was permitted to devote one of its elegant and very collectable editions to their own *Selected Poems* (2004), the pieces chosen by Alan Powers and the illustrations sensitively and amusingly provided by Peter Bailey.

By the year of Betjeman's death in 1984 the *Collected Poems* were in their fourth edition and so far had been reprinted in a size and style akin to the first edition of 1958, with *High and Low* added to the third

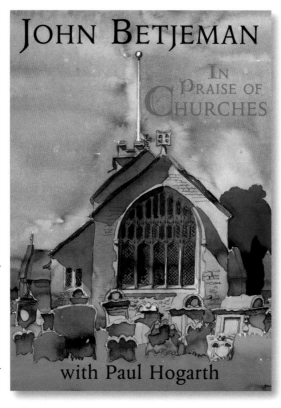

LEFT And an equally delightful book of church poems illustrated by the late Paul Hogarth.

FAR LEFT An attractive collection of his poems (1995) with illustrations by David Gentleman.

edition in 1970 and *A Nip in the Air* added to the fourth edition in 1980. In 1988 the collection was entirely reset with a larger page size and, for his ageing adherents, a more readable type size. There was also a rather unattractively bound 'de luxe' edition. By 2003 the careful exploitation of the poems initiated and maintained by 'Jock' Murray (and following a takeover of one of London's few surviving family publishers) the very personal touch was supplanted by less discriminating commercialism and a section of the general public who were presumed unwilling to pay £12.99 for the latest paperback edition of *Collected Poems*, containing 230 or so items (about 5.5p a poem), and further presumed not to have the wit to make their own choice of favourites, were offered *The Best-Loved Poems of John Betjeman*, also in paperback – which worked out at 70 titles for £8.99 (12.8p a poem).

All these pleasant and diverting publishing vagaries have left us with what we should gratefully see as a welcome surfeit of Betjeman in print. The general reader, probably 99% of his audience, may well feel that there are more than enough titles. But the avid student of Betjeman will not be satisfied until a scholarly hand is put to providing a truly 'Complete' edition with all the early poems, unprinted poems, late discoveries, and so on, included. Betjeman, if anyone, deserves such an accolade and not only for his poetical output but everything else he wrote.

JB And
The Anthologies

Francis Turner
PALGRAVE

THE
GOLDEN
TREASURY

With a fifth book selected by
JOHN PRESS

T he poetry anthology plays a key role in the establishment of literary reputations. Yet neither the history of anthologies nor a well–documented consideration of their importance has been wholeheartedly attempted. Probably the best known anthology in English literature is *The Golden Treasury of the Best Songs and Lyrical Poems in the English Language* edited by Francis Turner Palgrave in 1861 with much good advice from the compiler's friend Alfred, Lord Tennyson. The first edition included no living poets and missed out many not then considered worthy of the accolade of inclusion. Later editions widened their scope and even admitted living poets. John Betjeman found himself in *The Golden Treasury* in an edition with additional poems selected by Cecil Day Lewis in 1954, and continued there in an Oxford edition edited by John Press in 1965. It was Palgrave's bold use of the adjective 'best' to describe his choice that gave such prestige to the inclusion. Since then the making of anthologies has boomed and the output continues unabated; some of a fairly trivial and selective nature, but others, coming from academic and prestigious publishers, selected by influential scholars and eminent writers, have continued to play an important role in establishing the chosen poets as educational and household favourites.

Betjeman has always been well favoured in this respect and hardly an anthology appears in the present day without the appearance of at least one of the 250 or so poems that he has published. In 1997 a survey revealed that in a cross section of anthologies taken at the time his most-often anthologised poem was *A Subaltern's Love-song* with 70 entries, followed by *Christmas* with 53, *with Hunter Trials, Pot-Pourri in a Surrey Garden, Death in Leamington, In a Bath Teashop, In Westminster Abbey, How To Get on in Society, Business Girls, Seaside Golf and Indoor Games Near Newbury* all vying for third place in the '30s. This may not be the final reckoning of relative poetical value but it does offer a measure of the poem's popularity.

His first anthology appearance was in *Public School Verse: Vol. 5 1924-25* which heralded his future career as a poet just as he had become an Oxford undergraduate in 1925. The poem included was of no great distinction but an appearance in a real anthology published by a major publisher (Heinemann) was doubtless very satisfying at the time. Old friends can be of considerable importance in the anthology world, and his first notable poetry anthology entry was in *The Oxford Book of Light Verse* chosen by university chum W. H. Auden in 1938. The *Light* part of the title may not have been entirely welcome but Betjeman was also thanked in the introduction for 'many valuable suggestions,' and he was one of a small handful of living poets included. Auden, modestly, did not

ABOVE The poet leaves his London retreat at 43 Cloth Fair.

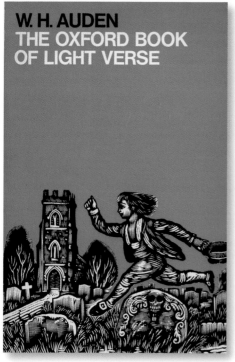

ABOVE
An important
appearance was in
*The Oxford Book of
Light Verse* (1938)
edited by his Oxford
friend W.H.Auden.

include himself. In 1938 he also had one poem in *The Year's Poetry,* somewhat oddly chosen as it was *The Wykehamist* written in 1931.

Inclusion in an anthology is often a most effective advert for a writer certainly if, like Betjeman, he has a distinctive style. A traditional and light-hearted sort of poem like *Dorset* stood out boldly in Ann Ridler's *A Little Book of Modern Verse* (graced with an introduction by T. S. Eliot) in 1941 where it was vying with the works of the modernist school of the 30s. In the same year he had two poems – *The Wykehamist* and *Upper Lambourne* in *A New Anthology of Modern Verse: 1920-1940* chosen by C. Day Lewis and L. A. G. Strong – a prestigious appearance with JB well aware of the importance (as mentioned earlier) of such inclusions as well as sensibly appreciating a future source of a small but regular revenue. One of his earliest American appearances (*Distant View of a Provincial Town*) was in *A Treasury of British Humour* in 1942, followed by a share of the influential popularity of *Great Modern Reading* edited by W. Somerset Maugham in 1943 which included *In Westminster Abbey*. It was good to be included amongst so many 'great' writers.

Although it is pleasant to be included in the more colourful anthologies like *Landmarks* edited by G. Rostrevor Hamilton and John Arlott (an influential promoter of poetry on radio) – and no less than four poems included; it is also remarkable that less reviewed educationally slanted volumes that regularly included him in the '40s and '50s, such as *Poems of To-Day* (Macmillan), were particularly useful as reputation builders – presenting poems to young and open minds that may well retain the memory of them throughout their lives.

Over the ensuing years the number of appearances steadily grew and it would be impossible to mention them all. Their patronage continued to serve on various levels. There were the important collections like *The New Oxford Book of Light Verse* chosen by Kingsley Amis in 1978 with seven Betjeman poems included and, even more generous, *The Oxford Book of Twentieth-Century English Verse* chosen by Philip Larkin in 1973 with twelve Betjeman items. Both again demonstrating enthusiastic support from old friends. The academic volumes were valuable testimonials, while a regular place in the popular family-oriented sort of anthologies such as those produced by John Hadfield in his *Books of* series – *Beauty* (1952), *Delights* (1954), *Britain* (1956), *Love* (1958), *Pleasures* (1960) and *Joy* (1962) did much to widen his popular appeal, as did several numbers of Hadfield's lavishly produced *Saturday Book*.

Betjeman was, of course, ideally available for any marauding hand that wanted to put together a subject anthology on anything ranging from horses to the festive season, guaranteeing regular appearances for *Hunter Trials*, *Advent* and *Christmas*. All this may sound a bit cosy, but the outlook is balanced by critical support as found in *The Times*, 'John Betjeman has succeeded better than most of his contemporaries in narrowing the gulf between poetry and the public. In his own province of feeling he has established a personal regency over all contemporary taste.' *Punch,* 'It would be difficult to point to a contemporary poet of greater originality or more genuine depth of feeling,' and from Philip Larkin, 'He is in the best sense a committed writer

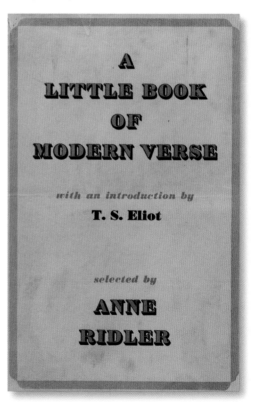

A LITTLE BOOK OF MODERN VERSE

with an introduction by

T. S. Eliot

selected by

ANNE RIDLER

whose poems spring from what he really feels about life, and as a result he brings back to poetry a sense of dramatic urgency it had all but lost.' All these are comments harvested from the back cover of *Collected Poems*. Even those who did not entirely share the general enthusiasm for his work, such as Geoffrey Grigson and John Wain, felt obliged to include him in various collections they made.

Betjeman was a noteworthy anthologist himself, producing several collections of high quality, taste and interest including *English, Scottish and Welsh Landscape* with Geoffrey Taylor in 1944, *English Love Poems* (1957) also with Taylor who died just before the book was published and received a warm tribute from JB, and *Altar and Pew* (1959).

Worth a special mention were certain anthologies that allowed poets to choose, from their own works, particular favourites or those they wished to be remembered by amongst their own poems. There were two outstanding examples of this line of approach. From the publisher George Harrap and edited by James Gibson, later a leading light in The Betjeman Society and even better-known from his scholarly work on the Dorset master Thomas Hardy, came *Let the Poet Choose* in 1973. Poets have commonly

ABOVE Betjeman made several appearances in the lavishly produced *Saturday Book*.

thought themselves to be misrepresented in anthologies either by persistent choice of the same poems – which is perhaps their fault if they have only written one or two memorable items – but they obviously want anthologists to widen their basis of acceptability – or if a wrong emphasis is given to their work. If the poet is asked to choose the chances are that he is going to give us an interesting and valuable insight into his tastes. It is not at all surprising that Betjeman did not go for the popular items like *Slough* or *In Westminster Abbey* but, in this instance, offered two deeper and more searching poems. He chose *Norfolk* and *Remorse* explaining, 'Some years ago I was visiting East Anglia when I suddenly found myself in a train going past the very place I'd spent so many weeks in when I was ten years old. I remembered those early days when everything seemed so exciting – and so full of hope. I've tried

to express in my poem, *Norfolk*, the feeling of those days compared with the feeling of guilt one has all the time now that one is older, the feeling that one has besmirched the wonderful opportunities that one has had. My second, *Remorse*, comes straight from the heart. It is about a death-bed scene at which I was present.' The real Betjeman in a nutshell, we might say – guilt, regret, sorrow, mingled with the evocative warmth of 'There after supper lit by lantern light / Warm in the cabin I could lie secure / And hear against the polished sides at night / The lap lap lapping of the weedy Bure'.

The other anthology of this kind is of American origin – *Poet's Choice* published by Dial Press and edited by Paul Engle and Joseph Langland in 1962. Here, perhaps for the benefit of an American audience he chooses an atypical Betjeman poem,

ABOVE Cartoon by Illingworth illustrating a Kenneth Allsop *Daily Mail* article in 1960.

one of the best of his exuberant tennis-playing girl kind of poems which he obviously enjoyed in spite of his accompanying gloss, 'I don't like any of my verses very much; only the one I am engaged on at the time interests me. I can see a certain skill in rhythm and use of words in *Pot-Pourri from a Surrey Garden*, as the verses, like all my verse, is meant to be recited out loud. The verses too imply the semi rural landscape of Surrey when strong girls play tennis and strong sons go to the right class of school for children of canasta-playing parents who live in half-timbered well-appointed villas among the conifers.'

Betjeman on Betjeman can be extended to various selections of his own verse he put together for use on radio and television. 'John Betjeman reads a selection of his own poetry', produced by Noel Iliff, was broadcast on the BBC Third Programme on 20 August 1949 and repeated on the 31st. He starts as elsewhere by affirming that:

'All the verse I have written was made to be read out loud. I shout it to myself time and time over, every line, hundreds of times over. I shout them when driving motor cars, walking in the streets or when I find myself in an empty railway carriage, and in this way I polish and re-polish stanzas and add internal rhymes to them which you may or may not notice when you heard them read… But I ought to warn you that my verse is of no interest to people who think. It jingles for the slaves of their own passions. On the obverse side, it is preoccupied with death; not a day passes without my visualising how I shall die and what will happen afterwards. So I've arranged the poems going from gay, through various passions to death – it gets more and more depressing as it goes on, this recital. First of all a topographical item; about a place; about that very little visited and most beautiful city of Bristol:

Poem: **Bristol** [originally 'A plain course on the bells']

Next one about a little tragedy that must be happening everywhere at this time of August – and that's when people come back from their holidays – small children especially. They go back to some noisy and drab suburb and they try to remember the sea they have just left and try to find the sea again in the noises they are now hearing. This I wrote about coming back from Cornwall and returning to Metroland. It's a little bit in the mood of A. A. Milne transferred from exclusive Kensington or Chiswick streets to Metroland – Wembley and around there.

Poem: **A Child's Lament** [*Harrow-on-the-Hill*]

BELOW
A lively American anthology compiled by the humorist Ogden Nash (1961).

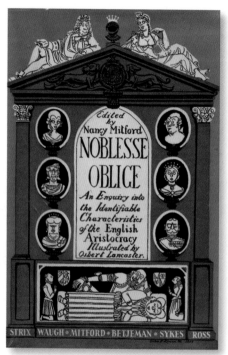

ABOVE The trendy *Noblesse Oblige* (Hamish Hamilton, 1956) was a good home for the much-anthologised *How To Get On In Society*.

Then from that first love of Cornwall and the sea one moves to the rather more conventional and lustful, I regret to say; lustful poems about great strapping sports girls whom I always see as being very beautiful. Added to these, in this poem, is the background beauty of Surrey – you know, conifers and tennis-courts and that kind of thing which has always seemed to me one of the charms of the English countryside, especially near London. And those girls playing among the conifers.

Poem: **Pot-pourri from a Surrey garden**

After that comes the feeling of guilt that one should really write that kind of poetry, if poetry you call it. I wrote a poem which is rather depressing called *Senex* about the sense of horror at being so moved by physical beauty only.

Poem: **Senex**

And after that, so to speak, purging of lust from the elements – the parts that make up love – there was this little poem about the Midlands of Ireland, and it's a love poem there imagined in the person of an Irish rake who was in love with a beautiful colleen, and it's, I like to think, less in the lustful mood of the former poems.

Poem: **Sir John Piers –2: The Attempt**

After that, as one gets older one feels that there is no chance of having that sort of love affair again, although love still plays a large part in my poetry writing. When I was convalescing with some friends down on the Beaulieu River a few years ago, I saw the most lovely girl go past in a 'sharpie' – you know, a sharpie's one of those little boats, sailing boats, that they use on Beaulieu River – and I thought, well, there's no chance of her ever loving me so I shall put myself into – her name was Clemency, by the way – I shall put myself into the position of some old lady sitting by the riverside and seeing her go by.

ABOVE An early 20th century picture of Harrow-on-the-Hill.

Poem: **Youth and Age on Beaulieu River**

Then there's one which gives, I hope, the purging effect of love and notices how the most dreary looking people are transformed by love and raised up by it. It is rather, I fear, a crib of Hardy, this poem, and it's a thing I saw that happened in a Bath teashop. [*In fact Betjeman later confessed that he was the 'thumping crook' and the*

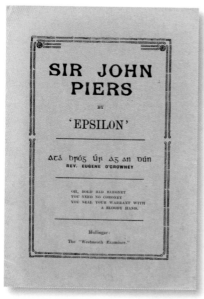

SIR JOHN
PIERS

BY

'EPSILON'

Αϲά ϧϼός ừϼ Δϛ Δn Ⅾún
REV. EUGENE O'GROWNEY

OH, BOLD BAD BARONET
YOU NEED NO CORONET
YOU SEAL YOUR WARRANT WITH
A BLOODY HAND.

Mullingar:
The "Westmeath Examiner."

ABOVE *Sir John Piers* was privately printed by The Westmeath Examiner, Mullingar in 1938 in a limited edition of 250, all hand-corrected by Betjeman. It contained six Irish poems greatly admired by Auden.

OPPOSITE: Bath in all its glory.

girl a BBC secretary he was having tea with during some filming in Bath. He continued to correspond with her].

Poem: **In a Bath Teashop**

So to the last thing, my preoccupation with death. It's always nice to be taken seriously, you know, and I like to think that this poem might be taken more seriously than most. It's called *Before the Anaesthetic* or *A real fright*. What had happened to me at the time is what happens to a lot of people – I had an operation – not a very serious one, but, of course, I thought it was very serious – and you know how they stick a needle into you about half an hour before the op then you lie back and they wheel you along to the operating theatre. There they stick another needle in you and you go off at once. Well that's what happened to me. And after the first needle I was lying in the nursing home in Oxford and the bells of St. Giles's church nearby started practising, and there was a terrible sense of eternity as I waited for the operation, feeling rather dreamy and funny. I put down these emotions so far as I could in this poem when I was feeling better.

Poem: **Before the Anaesthetic** or **A Real Fright**

[*It is to be hoped here, as indeed in the rest of the book, that readers will have a collection of Betjeman poems to hand for reference*]

By the end of his career in 1984 his poems must have appeared in several hundred anthologies – and many after. Since his death there has been something of a boom in anthology making, greatly promoted by popular poetry programmes on radio which, like similar productions on TV, make a popular thing of the competitive element. *The Nation's Favourite Poems* (1996) brought together 'the results of the poll in a collection of the nation's 100 best-loved poems.' At least it ends with a list chosen by people who regularly and voluntarily read or listen to poetry, rather than the academics, and the Betjeman devotee should be pleased that, in the face of

LITTLE BOOK OF **BETJEMAN**

such stern competition as Shakespeare and Tennyson and a generally strong field, Betjeman ended with two poems (matching Shakespeare who also had two) out of the allotted hundred. At No.1 came Rudyard Kipling with *If*, followed by Tennyson with *The Lady of Shalott*. Betjeman came in at No.62 with *Diary of a Church Mouse* and at No.70 with *Christmas*.

If that sort of anthologising gives pleasure to those with a competitive nature there are also many personal collections that give an added pleasure by offering an interesting insight into the minds of their compilers as well, showing interesting paths to follow that their discerning instincts have discovered. Such an anthology was a slim volume *If Love Be Love* compiled by the actor Rex Harrison in 1979 – full of unusual things and reflecting the compiler's wit and charm. Betjeman was represented therein by *A Subaltern's Love-song*. Another, from America, alive with good humour, as you might expect, was *Everybody Ought to Know* selected and introduced by Ogden Nash in 1961. This also included *A Subaltern's Love-song* along with *Trebetherick*. Naturally we are interested in well-known anthologists whose names add prestige and lustre. Among those with a special insight to offer were David Cecil's *Library Looking Glass* (1975) – with fascinating notes added, Kingsley Amis's *The Amis Anthology* (1988) and, with a specialist appeal, A. L. Rowse's *A Cornish Anthology* (1968). These were compiled by friends of Betjeman and naturally include an interesting choice of his poems.

With so many anthologies to choose from it

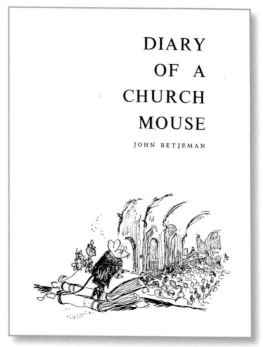

LEFT Betjeman on the trail of something or other in London.

BELOW A reprint of *Diary of a Church Mouse* as a fundraiser for Dorchester Abbey (1972).

DIARY
OF A
CHURCH
MOUSE

JOHN BETJEMAN

becomes impossible to pick an unarguable list of *the* best. But for pleasurable browsing there is nothing to surpass a good collection and the interest of finding the poet of one's choice in the context of his peers and betters.

To try to explain the particular appeal of a well-loved writer is even more difficult than explaining the attraction of a place or building. Betjeman's poetry complicates our problem by being on so many levels. Essentially he is a natural versifier and a rhyming man. Many of his poems are based on older poems that have caught his fancy or even hymns. When he was making his reputation he was a lone figure in the modernist field, unashamedly using propulsive metres and rhythms when so many were trying to make these archaic fundamentals less obvious. As already observed, he openly declared that he found rhyme a constant source of inspiration. It was a part of the magic of poetry; the growth of a line from the necessity to rhyme, the rhyme creating the thought – though better thought of if it could disguise this fact by the apparent timeless inevitability of the result. You could say that Betjeman wrote the sort of poetry that many amateur poets produce so badly, doing it with immense natural skill; a skill for inner and outer rhymes, unfailing scansion, the imaginative choice of word, originality of thought and honest commitment to truthful feelings.

A poem can be and clearly is often written on the basis of a single thought which is so expanded and handled that it ends up in an unforgettable shape. Let us take, as an example, a perfect and concise lyric poem such as *Harrow-on-the-Hill*. The poet has frequently explained how this is intended to capture the moment when somebody, most likely a young person, has returned to the ordinariness of his suburban life after a holiday in a favourite spot and

LEFT Novelist Kingsley Amis (1922-1950) was one of a younger generation who moved into Betjeman circles and anthologised his verse.

BELOW A very limited edition, written and illustrated by the poet in 1962.

his imagination transforms the drabness around him into a memory of the recently enjoyed seaside. He chooses a place in Metroland and finds Harrow-on-the-Hill. Betjeman never lived there or had any special connection so he clearly chose it as one of those lilting names (like Joan Hunter Dunn) which, in this case, stamps itself on the poem in the line *Then Harrow-on-the-Hill's a rocky island*. He would clearly have produced a very different poem had it been Walton-on-Thames (or Slough) that came to mind. The poem which seems so easy on the ear and mind is actually full of deft touches, like a good tennis player's improvised strokes. 'When melancholy Autumn comes to Wembley' disturbs the ghost of Keats before plumping for Wembley – a place that few beyond Betjeman would think of bringing into their poetry, likewise the next line 'And electric trains are lighted after tea'. So many poets, when you think of it, want to assert either their masculinity or their femininity, whichever the case may be, but Betjeman was never afraid of being sentimental – *The poplars near the Stadium are trembly / With their tap and tap and whispering to me,'* then moving bluntly into the theme of the poem, 'Like the sound of little breakers / Spreading out along the surf-line / When the estuary's filling / With the sea.*

There are only three stanzas and each is organically different, the second with its repetition of 'Harrow' and the inner rhyme in 'And the constant click and kissing of the trolley buses hissing,' the third with its cleverly loose rhyming of 'Perivale' and 'under sail.' But we must stop this school exam approach for there is nothing worse for poetry than dissecting it in this way, like, as someone pointedly said, killing a bird to find out what made it sing so beautifully.

The same poem, in a minor way compared to some, underlines one of the problems with Betjeman which is simply the individuality of his references. There is nothing in *Harrow-on-the-Hill* to compare with the positive plethora

BELOW
Daymer Bay was JB's favourite holiday haunt and the scene of many poems.

FARTHINGHOE NORTHANTS 1968.

of brand names that infest some poems (*Middlesex*, for example) and which are, to some extent, only effective if you know what they were brand names of and perhaps actually used them yourself in earlier days. The problem only arises if you are not familiar with Wembley and its Stadium, Wealdstone, Kenton and Perivale on the one hand and with Padstow and that wonderful estuary that Betjeman so loved – and Pentire. That one name is magic if you know where and what it is and can picture its dominance in the picture of Betjeman's part of North Cornwall.

To appreciate Betjeman's poetry to the full, to get its full effect, you must surely take the trouble to provide your own visual footnotes; in other words, to go to the places that the poems portray. *Seaside Golf* is a good poem by any standards but it is twice as good if you have played your seaside golf at St. Enodoc.

The Prose Writer

RIGHT His first prose work, published by (Chapman & Hall, 1933) had a cover contrived by the author from various print samples.

No writer has ever made a good living out of simply writing poetry and possibly nine-tenths of Betjeman's output over the years was in prose of one shape or another – essays, criticism, radio and TV scripts. If it is true that his greatness lies in his poetry, his worth as a prose writer has perhaps suffered by the comparison. But he was always a good prose writer, a born essayist and wrote in a style and vocabulary that is a natural complement to his poetry. His prose, like his verse, was a natural extension of his character. Colourful, warm, humorous and honest. He always said what he thought and often his forthright opinions have annoyed and irritated many. He was most virulent in his attacks on architectural atrocities but, in fact, spent only a small part of his output in damning for he was a kindly critic, rarely spoke ill of a fellow writer, and his greatest effort was spent in praising and promoting the things he admired.

His first full-length book was *Ghastly Good Taste* published by Chapman & Hall in 1935. Like his early books of poems it was a distinctive Betjeman production with a cover designed by him from odd bits of type and printer's decorations. His original sketch for it fortunately survives, giving a clear clue as to his interest in such matters as print and illustration. The text is forthright in his adherence to the subtitle 'A depressing story of the rise and fall of English Architecture' and makes lively reading. Its glory, so Betjeman modestly claimed, was a 'beautiful folding ILLUSTRATION forty inches long specially drawn by Peter Fleetwood-Hesketh'.

One of the first substantial reviews was by Osbert Burdett in *The Architectural Review* where it was billed a 'Book of the Month'. Although the critic mildly criticised the author for not actually defining in so many words what he actually meant by 'ghastly good taste' he was able to define it himself as being the imposition of self-conscious and fashionable notions on well established traditions. He agreed with Betjeman that so many buildings, and especially new trends, were simply wrong because they lacked a sense of proportion in relation to their surroundings or had outlines or inner compartments that outraged our senses the moment we observed or entered. He particularly admired the opening chapter in which Betjeman presented the story of one house as it was altered by its occupying owners in accordance with the prevailing fashions, wherein the reader might learn more

about architectural history than in many academic textbooks. If the author left us with a sense of the confusion of tastes that indiscriminate building has left, so be it. It was all admirably presented and the first chapter along with Mr. Fleetwood-Hesketh's illuminating illustration made it the 'most original architectural essay' of

recent times.

Betjeman's natural talent lay not in full length prose works but in what were virtually extended essays. He had a flair for compressing historical perspective into a readable and illuminating survey imparting more insight than many a lengthier treatise on the same subject. His best writing on his pet subject of churches came in the introduction to *Collin's Guide to English Parish Churches* which eventually came out in 1958, having been first discussed in 1947 and commissioned in 1950 and long a source of anxiety to its publisher and stress to its editor over the years. The rest of the book, only partly by Betjeman who wrote on only a handful of counties that most interested him, leaving the rest to friends and colleagues, contains other good introductory pieces but, on the whole, is too perfunctory in its treatment of the majority of churches. It survives on the merits of Betjeman's discerning Introduction.

A piece of similar insight and purpose is the lively essay he contributed to *Flower of Cities*, a collection of 22 pieces on London published by Max Parrish in 1949. Betjeman covers all the main railway stations in a 17-page piece and leaves one wishing for more. Later he brought together a series of essays on individual London stations which he had contributed to

LEFT Architectural musing and a helpful cigarette in the 1930s.

FAR LEFT A tasteful collection of essays published by Max Parrish in 1949 included an adroit Betjeman piece on 'London Railway Stations'.

Wheeler's Review from 1968 to 1970. *London's Historic Railway Stations*, published by Murray in 1972 was a book full of episodic delights and well deserved an expanded reprint in 2002. We come to realise that Betjeman is not only essentially a poet writing prose, but writing it in the length and proportions of a poem and reliant upon a good head of inspiration to keep it going.

By the same token his best prose book is still the book of essays, articles and broadcasts brought together by his friend Myfanwy Piper in 1952 under the title *First and Last Loves*. Unforgettably romantic and poetical are pieces such as he wrote on such churches as Blisland in Cornwall and St. Mark's in Swindon. There is little doubt here that he was essentially an essayist in the prose field, made to operate in short burst of inspiration, and able to produce such bursts as a working journalist week after week as in the pieces he wrote for *The Spectator* under the title of *City and Suburban* from 1954 to 1958. Such pieces began to find their way into anthologies alongside the poems and his talent for prose was finally recognised in the large collection assembled by his daughter Candida Lycett Green in *Coming Home*, published by Methuen in 1997. The recognition had taken a long time since the perhaps unexpected appearance of a piece called *England Revisited*, culled from *The Listener*, in what was essentially one of an educational series – *Modern Essays* – Volume 2 published by Macmillan in 1944.

To make a brief list of Betjeman's published books of prose is to compile a dossier of strange, varied, delightful and variable oddments with most of them well worth a visit. They interestingly include two Shell Guides – *Cornwall* (1934) and *Devon* (1936) and one in collaboration with John Piper – *Shropshire* (1951); the eccentric book about Oxford which Oxford might not have expected – *An Oxford University Chest* (1938); *Antiquarian Prejudice* (1939); *Vintage London* (1942); *English Cities and Small Towns* (1943); a study of *John Piper* (1944); *Murray's Buckinghamshire* (1948); *Murray's Berkshire* (1949) – both with John Piper; *The English Scene* – a reader's guide (1951); *The English Town in the Last Hundred Years* – Rede Lecture (1956); *English Churches* (with Basil Clarke) (1964); *The City*

An Oxford University Chest

John Betjeman

LEFT An early prose work *An Oxford University Chest* (1938) reprinted in 1979.

of London Churches (1965); *A Pictorial History of English Architecture* (1972); *West Country Churches* – 4 essays (1973) and a delightful children's book, *Archie and the Strict Baptists* (1977) which upset some Baptists at about the same time as the 'Jubilee Hymn' controversy. While none of these compare in importance and impact with his best books of poems, they are a valuable complement to a study of what made this most intriguing man tick.

The Journalist

For all of his working life John Betjeman was a journeyman writer, a hack journalist – or the equivalent in terms of the modern medium of broadcasting. This meant an unremitting round of writing what one might not at any particular moment want to write and, although grumbling most of the time about the demands thrust upon him – and how little he was paid for his labours, turning out the goods to a pretty high standard of excellence – if not always of the inspirational order required of a poem. As the demands upon him increased he admitted that he would never have been able to cope with the work had it not been for the help and devotion of a series of efficient and, usually, attractive secretaries on whom he could develop harmless crushes. Outstanding amongst this succession of young ladies was Jill Menzies, his secretary from 1954 to 1959 who was the type that most set his heart a-flutter and who he fondly referred to as 'Freckly Jill'. Possibly feeling that the crush was getting too much to handle or simply looking for a better future than attending to the needs of a demanding middle-aged poet, Freckly Jill left his service in 1959 leaving him broken-hearted and in need of a suitable replacement. Anita Dent was the lady chosen – equally efficient if not as dear to his heart – which was probably a good thing. The last service which Freckly Jill performed was to write a lengthy memo to her successor to help her settle into the routine as easily as possible, and it gives a very clear idea of how Betjeman employed his working hours at that time:

'Type letters and file them, including letters Mr. Betjeman will bring up from Wantage every week.

Keep a diary of engagements, lectures etc., and write down fees received for such

THE JOURNALIST

lectures in the diary so that they can be added up for income tax return.

Keep an account of petty cash spent on office oddments and stamps in the diary, again for income tax.

Keep a list in front of File 6 "Literary Work" of articles etc. which Mr. Betjeman has agreed to do, again with fees written down so that these can be added up. Remind him when it is time to write and send in an article.

File odd bills for garage repairs, petrol, stationery, drink, etc. in small accounts file, but all other accounts go in the appropriate file.

Look after Mr. Betjeman's insurance book. Put in a stamp for 7/5d each week and see that the card is sent in to be changed when it is filled. Get the 7/5d (and half your own insurance) from Mr. Betjeman. The easiest way is to get him to add it to your cheque.

229 STRAND

The office of
THE LONDON MERCURY
*No. 229 Strand is one of the very few seventeenth century
buildings remaining in the four mile radius and stands immediately
opposite the Law Courts*

Order new stationery when necessary. Octave die-stamped writing paper and die-stamped typing paper, and court octavo "Bodleian Ivory" envelopes are ordered from Messrs. Emberlin and Son, 4 Lincoln House, Turl Street, Oxford. You can order these yourself on Mr. Betjeman's behalf, signing yourself Secretary to Mr. John Betjeman. Half the stationery will have to be kept in London and half in Wantage, as Mr. B. hopes to have someone to do letters here part time at the end of the week. Also order foolscap bond typing paper, flimsy foolscap for copies, and lined foolscap writing paper for Mr. B. to write articles on. This at Emberlins too, or from the Swindon Typewriter Co. Ltd., 13 Bath Road, Swindon, Wilts., who come to inspect the typewriter once a quarter and are often over this way. I use old large envelopes with economy labels when necessary rather than buying new ones which are v. expensive. Get a typewriter hired in London for Warwick Avenue, and get the money out of Mr. B. for this.

The old typewriter will remain in Wantage. We have a contract with the Swindon Typewriter Co. who look after all repairs on it and come to inspect and clean it once a quarter in return for an annual payment. Order your typewriter ribbons in half dozens from them.

Mr. Betjeman's main work now is as follows:

Daily Telegraph

Once a fortnight he writes a review of new novels. This has to be handed in, or sent, to the *Daily Telegraph* on the Monday before the Friday when it is to appear; this means it has to be written and typed by the Saturday before. Usually Mr. Betjeman will take the review in to the *Daily Telegraph* himself every Monday: if he can't do this, you, or I suppose he, as you won't be there, will put it into the post on Saturday or Sunday. The weeks when this review is to be written are marked in the diary as "Review Week" (a dreadful time!). Books for review are chosen by Mr. B. every time he goes to the *Daily Telegraph* and sent to his home; they will be sent to Warwick Avenue in future. Undo the parcels of books when they arrive and put them all on a shelf, with little markers stuck into the backs on which is written the date when the books are to be published (no review can appear of a book before that date). When the books have been reviewed, or if Mr. B. decides he doesn't want to review the book, you will send them packed up in cardboard boxes, or any other safe way you like, to J. Clarke-Hall Ltd., Wine Office Court, Fleet Street, London, E.C.4.

BELOW The Betjeman signature went through many permutations.

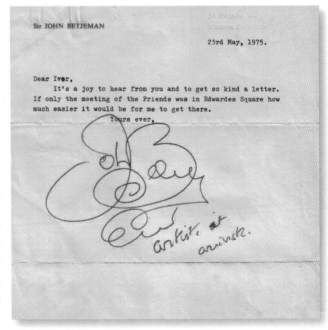

Sir JOHN BETJEMAN

23rd May, 1975.

Dear Iver,

It's a joy to hear from you and to get so kind a letter. If only the meeting of the Friends was in Edwardes Square how much easier it would be for me to get there.

Yours ever,

They give Mr. B. half the price for the books. They provide boxes with printed labels addressed to them; write Mr. B's name and address in the space at the top of the label, and you need not send any explaining letter in the parcel. When you run out of labels ask Clarke-Hall for some more.

Time and Tide

He is something rather vague on the staff of this weekly review which you have probably never read. He is "Literary Advisor" and arranges for people to write reviews of books and general articles in the book section: he has nothing to do with the political side (or "Whither Democracy Section" as he calls it). He goes to Time and Tide's offices (32, Bloomsbury Street, W.C.1., Museum 3855) once a week, usually on Monday afternoon. His secretary or helper there is called Pamela Fildes; ask for her if you ever have to telephone. You will have hardly anything to do with Time and Tide; if people ring you up or write about Time and Tide business, refer them to Miss Fildes at Time and Tide if Mr. B. is not about.

Punch

Mr. B. has lately taken to writing articles for Punch twice or three times a month. These will be written in the week which is not review week. Either you or the girl down here, if there is one, will type out the article when done (ditto the Daily Telegraph review). Proofs of all articles are sent to Mr. B. for correction. These should be returned corrected, except for the Daily Telegraph one of which the corrections must be telephoned immediately. Central 3232, and ask for Miss Grant (she is the assistant literary editor. The literary editor is called George Bishop, but he doesn't usually do such menial work as dealing with corrections).

BELOW Betjeman and other Laureates celebrated in Hampstead.

Celebrating poets laureate who have served Her Majesty Queen Elizabeth II

The Queen's Poets

LONDON METROPOLITAN ARCHIVES

John Keats
keats house
Hampstead London

THE JOURNALIST

RIGHT A working
journalist who
contributed to
many London and
provincial papers.

B.B.C.

Mr. B. used to do quite a lot of broadcasting, some for the Home Service, and some for the West Region stationed in Bristol. He has been trying to do less lately, in order to get his book for Collins on English Parish Churches finished. So try to keep him from accepting things. He is going to take some television work on architecture soon. George Barnes is the director of television at the B.B.C. and is a friend of Mr. B's.

Odd articles

He accepts things that are interesting and well-paid! Again try to keep him from accepting too much until his book is finished.

Book on English Parish Churches for Collins

This has been on contract for 9 years! It consists of a long introduction of a very general nature to English parish churches and the reason why they should be looked at. This is followed by chapters on each county in England, consisting of a short general introduction to the county and lists of the churches worth visiting. Mr. Betjeman's collaborator in the lists is Mr. E. T. Long, The Red House, Sherborne, Dorset, who is a hard-working and rather nice pedant, whose patience has been much tried by delays over the book. The main introduction and lists have been written, but Collins want a lot changed, and the thing will have to be completely overhauled.

Murray's Architectural Guide to Oxford

is the next book on the agenda, which must be done after the Church Book. Mr. B. should not take on anything else till this is done! Mr. John Grey Murray (otherwise Jock Murray) is Mr. B's publisher and personal friend. He is soon going to publish another book of Mr. B's poems: these have just been sent to Mr. B. for revision.

BELOW A booklet with collected radio tributes to churches in Swindon, Blisland and Mildenhall.

WEST COUNTRY CHURCHES
Four Essays
BY
JOHN BETJEMAN
Poet Laureate
1973
Society of SS. Peter and Paul,
7 Tufton Street, Westminster, S.W.1.
Price : Forty Pence

Poetry

Poems only get written occasionally. When one is written and has come to some fairly final form, make a lot of copies of it, and send one to Mr. John Murray. He keeps a complete set of all poems. There is a file for poems here; keep each poem and any relevant correspondence, various versions, etc. in a separate section.

There is also a drawer full of old bits and in which every scrap of paper containing a few lines, however messy, should be kept.

Cut out all

articles and poems from the publications in which they appear, as well as keeping copies, and file these, the articles, all together in front of No.6 "Literary Work", and the poems in their appropriate section of the poetry file. Keep a copy of B.B.C. talks in the front of the B.B.C. file, all together.

Petty Cash

You will not get a regular allowance of this. Ask Mr. B. for whatever money you want, keep an account of roughly in the diary. What he wants is not to be bothered about any of it! Buy about a pound's worth of stamps, ¾ of twopenny halfpenny, and about a quarter of twopenny and penny-halfpenny, each week. Just ask him for the money for this.'

(The Warwick Avenue referred to above was abandoned as a potential office as JB shortly moved into Cloth Fair, where Miss Dent was involved in a minor fire incident but seems to have survived in the post for some years).

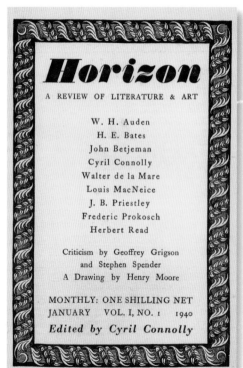

Horizon

A REVIEW OF LITERATURE & ART

W. H. Auden
H. E. Bates
John Betjeman
Cyril Connolly
Walter de la Mare
Louis MacNeice
J. B. Priestley
Frederic Prokosch
Herbert Read

Criticism by Geoffrey Grigson
and Stephen Spender
A Drawing by Henry Moore

MONTHLY: ONE SHILLING NET
JANUARY   VOL. I, NO. 1   1940

Edited by Cyril Connolly

His first and last full-time employment in professional journalism started in October 1930 when he became, at the behest of his friend Osbert Lancaster, assistant editor on The *Architectural Review* under the editorship of J. Cronin Hastings, a fairly lax employer who had to put up with some fairly irregular office hours but still got a fair amount of work out of JB including some excellent full length articles, reviews and occasional poems and a deal of anonymous work that still needs identifying. He left in the beginning of 1935 and thereafter remained basically a freelance author and broadcaster.

Having written an article on British 'Peers without Tears' which was published in the *Evening Standard* on 19 December 1933, and which pleased the paper's proprietor Lord Beaverbrook, he was offered the post of film critic to the paper starting in the following February. Betjeman's knowledge and experience of the film world must have been scant at the time but he stuck nobly to the task until 20 August 1935 when, in his final piece on the cinema, he confessed that the chore of providing several articles a week for two and a half years was bringing him near to the point of insanity.

BELOW One of his several well-written and knowledgeable books on architecture.

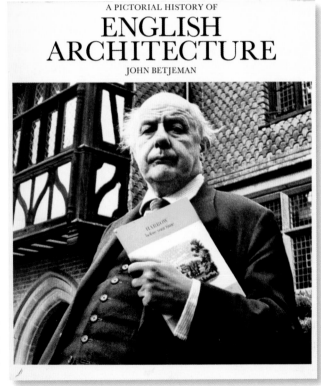

These chicks are too snobbish to play
With their poor little cousin. They say
"Young William, alas,
Is hardly our class;
He was never brought up on 'White May'."

WHITE MAY
PARAFFIN
FOR INCUBATORS
AND BROODERS
Write for our free poultry booklets to
Shell-Mex and B.P. Ltd., "White May" Poultry Technical Service
Shell-Mex House, Victoria Embankment, London, W.C.2
5838

ABOVE His employment with Shell in early days included writing advertising slogans and verses and editing the Shell Guides.

From August 1935 until 1939 he worked for the publicity department of the Shell Oil Company, where he wrote copy for adverts, produced films, and edited the popular Shell Guides.

A large proportion of his subsequent journalistic work was as a book critic, dealing with a vast range of literature - novels, essays, poetry, topography, architecture - and almost anything else that came along. He wrote for a number of magazines, well-known and otherwise. He wrote perceptively and truthfully on Stephen Leacock in *The Listener* (16 March 1939) - 'Leacock's humour is of the hit-and-miss type. It is the kind of humour we can grow out of; what seemed funny in our 'teens seems crude in our thirties. So it is, sometimes, with Leacock. He does not write satire, nor parody, nor pure nonsense, but a burlesque which is a mixture of all three' . . .'I feel that Leacock is best appreciated when one is feeling uncritical or recovering from 'flu and wanting something very light. Too much of him is too much for a sophisticated old decadent like JOHN BETJEMAN.'

On 16 September 1939 he was writing in the *New Statesman,* under the title 'Onwards from Dr.Watts' on Hilaire Belloc's *Cautionary Verses.* 'I doubt if there are better humorous verse writers in England than Mr. Belloc. He has all the quality needed - brevity, well-sounding lines, quotability, and simplicity. He is never facetious, never obscure, and he makes nice use of the unexpected.'

Wise observance from the variously talented man who was himself writing at this time *In Westminster Abbey* (New Statesman – 30 September 1939), and, in *The Architectural Review, The Seeing Eye or How To Like Everything.*

Although an industrious fellow he was not indefatigable and probably found the next prolonged chore as book-reviewer for *The Daily Herald* from 1943 to the end of 1947 a little demanding at times. Often he would rely on friends to read the duller books for him keeping the choicer items for himself. He set the scene on 11 October 1943 by saying in his introductory piece, 'Never have bookshops done better; never have they had more tripe to sell.' It was that strange time of war when one well-known author's manuscript was turned down because 'it would sell too well and we have not the paper to spare for a best-seller.'

Much of what he reviewed was commonplace. It is interesting to see how he appreciated and handled the occasional masterpieces that came his way. 17 November 1943: *Put Out More Flags* by Evelyn Waugh – 'People say he is a satirical writer. I always find him very much like the truth, only twice as entertaining.' 18 October 1944: *Four Quartets* by T. S. Eliot – 'There is little doubt that the greatest established poet writing in Britain today is T. S. Eliot. . . In *The Dry Salvages* (which he quotes at length) "anyone who loves the sea will surely feel the wind and heaving tide and hear the bell-buoy through the fog when he reads the lines out loud. As to obscurity, I would have said that there is none here." 4 September 1946: *Mainly on the Air* by Max Beerbohm, 'This book is high standard even for Max

ABOVE He was a contributor to the short-lived *Night and Day* and was also reviewed in its pages.

Beerbohm. What riches, what wit, what delicacy, what poetic recollection of a graceful past!'

After the *Herald*, from 1952 he reviewed for *The Daily Telegraph* and continued to do so for most of his writing life, but he always seemed to be a second-string reviewer there and rarely got the plum items. What became increasingly important were his basically 'topographical' items which he wrote for the *Telegraph* under the heading of *Men and Buildings* and these were thoughtfully and well written pieces, as if he realised his role and power as Britain's leading conservationist, and often splendidly illustrated by Leonora Ison. They were not in any way, perfunctory pieces, and he was

given plenty of space to expand his themes.

But perhaps the greatest body of regular journalistic writing that he achieved was to be found in *The Spectator* where, from 1954 to 1958 he wrote a weekly column, when not away or ill, under the title *City and Suburban*. For this he roamed the country far and wide and moved into a more popular kind of journalism, though always pointed and well-informed, delighting in such headings as 'Britain's Best Village' (Ashwell), 'the most beautiful town left in England' (Stamford), 'best market square, etc.' And he would regularly print a 'Casualty List' (or sometimes it was 'The Vandal's Register') of all the dark deeds of destruction and 'improvement' that town planners had perpetrated. It was a list that no-one wanted to be in.

The average reader could probably only dabble in the vast amount of 'journalism' that Betjeman left behind and much of it would take a lot of finding. Fortunately we have a splendid anthology of his prose writings selected and introduced by his daughter Candida Lycett Green under the title *Coming Home* (Methuen, 1997).

LEFT
The impressive Church of St.Mary's at Uffington. Betjeman's local.

ABOVE
Philip Larkin, old friend and admirer, at the Memorial Service in 1984.

Radio & TV

There is little doubt that much of Betjeman's popularity was built on his regular radio broadcasts and latterly on his television appearances which made him a well-known and well-loved celebrity and must have led many, who might not have done so otherwise, to sample his writings.

He was first heard on radio in 1932 giving his views on the fate of the old Waterloo Bridge. As with many of his subsequent talks this was backed by appearing in print in the BBC's influential weekly magazine *The Listener*. The majority of his talks in the thirties were on topographical subjects including the prototype 'How to Look at a Church' in August 1938, but mingled with pieces on music-hall, literary and architectural figures, turning more and more, into the forties, to literary topics and poetry programmes. He appeared on such panel programmes as Book Talk (1944) and amongst the ephemera would produces pieces that had an enduring quality like *Aberdeen Granite* (1947) and the appraisals of favourite churches such as Mildenhall, Swindon and Blisland which were preserved in *First and Last Loves* (1952), as were portraits of seaside towns such as Port Isaac, Bournemouth, Clevedon and Ilfracombe. By the time he made his last broadcast in 1980 he had made well over

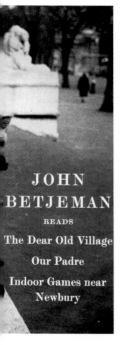

JOHN
BETJEMAN

READS

The Dear Old Village

Our Padre

Indoor Games near
Newbury

500 programmes. Many of these have been lost, as they were never kept in a permanent form, but quite a few survive and will hopefully be more researched and rediscovered in the future. Hearing Betjeman reading his poetry in a voice that was entirely suited to their content and style was the best way to get to know it and the same dedication and warmth came into most subjects that he touched upon.

He had made a brief appearance on the early TV screen in 1937 in a piece called How to Make a Guide Book. In 1959 he was seen reciting his poems against various London backgrounds, but it was not until the mid-Sixties that he took so naturally to the medium and began to produce a succession of TV classics. He was so natural, so warm, so involved and, always, so knowledgeable.

In 1964 there were three memorable films of him talking to Philip Larkin. In 1970 an informative series on Victorian Architects and Architecture which made many people familiar for the first time with names he idolised such as Comper, Lutyens and Norman Shaw, and a notable visit to the Isle of Man. In 1971 a perceptive series on the English landscape as seen from a helicopter (Betjeman preferring to stay on the ground) and in 1972 his very memorable series made in Australia with producer Margaret McCall. With the likeable man who became his TV Boswell, Jonathan Stedall, he produced two masterpieces in 1972 called *Thank God It's Sunday* which gave a new slant to off the cuff TV. In 1973 his generally acknowledged TV masterpiece *Metro-Land* as artfully put together by the inspired producer Edward Mirzoeff. There is an immediacy and appeal about this film that never loses its hold and scenes such as where JB misses his teeing-off shot at Moor Park or where he listens to the maestro of the Wurlitzer in Chorley Wood are unforgettable. Betjeman's eminent TV career can be fully sampled and appreciated in the splendid compilation that Jonathan Stedall

MIDDLE In the 1950s and thereafter the Betjeman voice was regularly recorded.

THE POET LAUREATE
Sir John Betjeman's Britain

1977

Music by Jim Parker

ABOVE One of the series of Jim Parker Charisma recordings.

put together in 1983 – *Time Out With Betjeman* – combining new material shot in Radnor Walk and Cornwall with clips from many of his memorable BBC films. A number of valuable items from independent TV sources, once thought to be lost, were retrieved in two Video/DVD compilations *The Lost Betjemans* and *Betjeman Re-Visited*.

Beyond the radio and TV items there has been a good sampling of the poet recording his own poems and, occasionally, the work of other writers. An Argo LP (actually the second) made in June 1959 has been in and out of the listings in various forms but will probably survive the years with definitive readings of some of his best-known pieces, supplemented by the Argo recording of *Summoned by Bells* made in November 1961. The BBC has also issued a collection of his readings from various broadcasts, both poems and prose.

Four recordings made by Charisma Records in 1974 have Betjeman reading his poems against a delightful musical background written by Jim Parker. While the combination sometimes succeeds there are also instances when either the poet reads in a slightly stilted sort of way as if distracted by the music or, on the other foot, when the listener is distracted from the poetry by the jovial music-making that sometimes competes with rather than complements the verse. Opinions vary greatly as to the ultimate success of this venture but there are many who find the experience entirely pleasing.

Setting verse to music particularly well-known verse has always been a matter for heated discussion. The answer to the problem is probably that the composer is best served by poems that in themselves are slight and undemanding. Schubert, one of the greatest songwriters of all time, generally chose poems of this nature. There were also poets who knew how to write a suitable lyric and always foremost amongst these was William Shakespeare who had a natural understanding of music's requirements and how the metre and rhythm should be varied to avoid monotony as well as how the words should be kept songlike and uncomplicated if their sense is not to be lost. We must come to the conclusion that Betjeman's poems, unlike, say, Houseman's, are not ideally suited to song-setting. There is too much going on in them, too many subtleties that can be lost, often too much inbuilt rhythm of their own. The sad fact remains that the composers who have attempted Betjeman settings [they include Mervyn Horder, Madeleine Dring, Donald Swann, Malcolm Williamson, and Mike Read] have not had any outstanding success and most attempts have been failures to varying degrees. These poems are not for setting.

BELOW
As presenter of the ABC 'Bookman' programme 6 September 1960 with editor Kenneth Young, David Daiches, Elizabeth Jane Howard and John Braine. *Photo Mark Gerson.*

The Preservationist

'He has established a personal regency over contemporary taste.' *The Times*

While most of the general public, if asked about John Betjeman, might know that he was primarily a poet, quite a few might well remember him as that chap who was always going around saving old buildings. Which would, of course, be greatly over-simplifying his activities in this direction. At the peak of his activities as a conservationist he was receiving around 50 letters a day asking for his advice and help on such matters.

Being pre-eminently a lover of churches it would hardly be surprising to find him rallying to the cause if anyone proposed to knock down a decent church. When such vandalistic thoughts occur they tend to be from within the church establishment rather than coming from outside speculators. One of the most notable furores into which Betjeman plunged was when the keepers of Holy Trinity Church, Sloane Street, Chelsea proposed in 1974 to demolish the existing magnificent and unusual building and replace it with a smaller church that would be part of a commercial development in a rich area for property developers. Oddly enough, at the time there was no legal protection for such buildings that were in working use, so someone had to come in with a point of view that had more to do with posterity and aesthetics than blatant commercialism. Of course, as in all such cases, there may have been some argument against keeping a church that was perhaps under-used and expensive to maintain. It had been badly damaged in the blitz in 1941 and it was never fully restored. Betjeman had already written a poem about the church in 1939, and had his own vested interest, but he pointed out in strong terms its tremendous merits as a cathedral of the Arts and Crafts movement with work by such artists as Sir Edward Burne-Jones and used his laureate pen once again to good effect. A booklet *A Plea for Holy Trinity Church, Sloane Street* was produced with four drawings by Gavin Stamp and an impassioned introduction by JB. As the church did not want to support the appeal, Betjeman and Stamp saw to it that the booklet was widely circulated and Betjeman put the seal on the campaign by publishing a new poem in the *Sunday Times* on 15 September 1974.

There is a whole book to be written on his campaigns. Amongst the successful and remembered were the halting of a ghastly plan to build a multi-storeyed hotel in the Avon Gorge at Bristol which would have obscured both the view and the famous suspension bridge; the widening of Maiden Lane in London which would have entailed the destruction of that celebrated restaurant known as Rules, the demolition of St. Pancras Station and the Criterion Theatre,

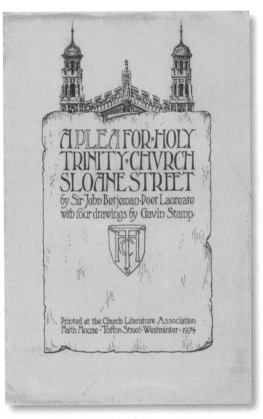

affrays ranging from major to minor affairs like the closure of Dilton Marsh Halt in Somerset – a short single platform where intending passengers could hold up their brollies to stop and board the train – a campaign that not only aroused great press interest over a wide time, but came to symbolise authoritarian interference with the nation's railways, and also produced an oft-quoted poem among the train-loving element of JB admirers – of which there are many. Betjeman travelled far and wide on railways but it is probably true to say that he was more interested in stations than

ABOVE Amongst Betjeman's notable if lesser deeds of preservation was the keeping open of the small railway halt at Dilton Marsh.

trains. The Liverpool Street Station campaign ended with a compromise solution which allowed some modern improvements but kept the old train shed and is now at least kept in great condition. Then there were the piers – a special interest of his as well as 'peers' – Southend and Clevedon were amongst his successes here – the list of his triumphal campaigns could be as long as the piers themselves. The West Pier in Brighton was saved by an energetic campaign but was later allowed to fall into the sea – so only a partial success. Churches, of course, by the dozens. Including several Hawksmoor churches in the City of London. St. Mary-le-Strand for which as a fund-raiser JB produced a rather humdrum poem which was printed and sold. He went to Stoke Poges to raise money for the Thomas Gray sarcophagus. The famous old Royal Agricultural Hall in Islington which survived to become a Business Design Centre. His local landmark – the White Horse at Uffington. The home of Richard Jefferies near Swindon. Supporting a great lifetime interest he supported the campaign to save Wilton's Music Hall in the East End. He was still in full battle-order as late as the early 1980s.

There were, of course, the failures. Notably, in London, Euston Station and its

ABOVE Another church saved was the unique St.Katherine's, Chiselhampton, Oxon. in 1972.

famous Arch which was last spotted as a heap of masonry in a Kentish builder's back garden, and a cast-iron masterpiece, The Coal Exchange. Betjeman's eloquence may have failed on many occasions but it succeeded on many more. He never seemed to grudge the time given for a worthy cause. A small volume could be published containing just his letters to *The Times*.

A Letter Or Two

Between his ongoing journalistic assignments: film and book reviewing, his work for radio, television and recording companies, the many books to be written and compiled, giving lectures, and the endless travel involved, he kept up a staggering flow of letters. Even if many of them were actually typed out

by secretaries, the majority were, as he preferred in his old fashioned way, hand–written – not entirely an advantage as his handwriting was notoriously illegible. The number, now occupying many filing cabinets in academic institutions, is simply staggering. In two exciting volumes perceptively introduced and selected by his daughter Candida we find letters that were never dull, always deeply concerned with their recipients, as full of thought and imagination as his professional writings. As a revealing example of the complexities of his life and how he worked, this is a letter written to his publisher friend Jock Murray in 1973.

'Dear Jock,

   I now enclose the completed sonnet on 'Back from Australia'. The sextet of which Thomas Edward Driberg and I worked out two evenings ago. I think it an improvement.

   I also enclose the completed Princess Anne poem of which the first three stanzas have been sent to the Queen and acknowledged. I rather dread having to write to the Prince of Wales about the Investiture poem. It will involve getting in touch with courtiers. Except for Patrick Plunkett they are rather stuffed shirts when it comes to granting favours. I think the best way to go about it if you want to print the poem is to write to me asking for it or part of it and then I can enclose the letter. How difficult life is. You should certainly get a superb book compiled by Lady Elizabeth Basset called 'Love is My Meaning': 'An Anthology of Assurance', Darton, Longman and Todd. Yours in need of assurance,

   As always
   John'

LEFT The grave at St.Enodoc with its fancifully inscribed headstone.

BELOW A little-known Betjeman recording made in 1960.

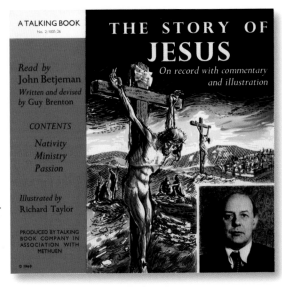

A TALKING BOOK
No. 2/1005:26

THE STORY OF
JESUS
On record with commentary
and illustration

Read by
John Betjeman
Written and devised
by Guy Brenton

CONTENTS

Nativity
Ministry
Passion

Illustrated by
Richard Taylor

PRODUCED BY TALKING
BOOK COMPANY IN
ASSOCIATION WITH
METHUEN

© 1960

Epilogue

Some verses written by Roger Woddis (who so often enjoyed himself and amused others by parodying Betjeman) written to herald the showing of *Time With Betjeman* in 1983, express some of the reactions that the world has had to Betjeman's poetry in a gentle but positive way:

" Young in his seventy-seventh year, and open,
    For all its ills, to all the world's delights,
His public stance a private view of Chelsea,
    He practises his careful craft and writes.

The raging storms beyond his study window.
    Seem no more real than slogans on a wall;
The outer life of telegrams and anger
    Professedly concern him not at all.

He has a passion for Victoriana,
    Nostalgia flows like lava from his quill;
How lovely the remembered dreams of Cornwall!
    How long the golden days of Muswell Hill!

Yet there's an imp that perches on his shoulder,
    A heart not fully broken on his sleeve;

The tennis tomboys and the hockey charmers
    Are fantasies we only half-believe.

But when he writes of lonely girls in Camden,
    Or fearful patients in a cheerless ward,
The easy voice turns into something darker,
    and strikes a deep and universal chord.'

LEFT One of the few plaques up to date is the one at Cloth Fair.

BELOW In a TV quiz show 'My Word' with Gilbert Harding and Nancy Spain in 1955. Cartoon and review in *Punch*.

Betjeman always had adverse critics, some of whom, in their role as anthologist, felt bound to include him in their collections without actually liking what he wrote. Those such as Geoffrey Grigson come to mind, who generously promoted him while feeling honour bound to write in his *Recollections* (1984), 'Do I believe, as I have been told, that after some earlier pinprick Betjeman climbed from his house at Uffington and cursed me from the backside of the White Horse? Why not? John Betjeman showed himself a kindly and forgiving man; but I detested and still detest his verses, or most of them.' A. L. Rowse, in his copy of the book with these words within, a firm admirer of Betjeman, pencilled in 'Envy of JB' and summed up the whole of *Recollections* as 'A nasty book by a nasty man. The nastiest book I have ever encountered.'

Some of the most adverse comments came with the publication of *Summoned by Bells* and Betjeman was deeply hurt by them. John Wain in *The Observer* wrote under the cutting heading of A SUBSTITUTE FOR POETRY and spoke of its 'pathetic inadequacy'. It is only fair to mention that he had been an admirer of Betjeman's earlier poems and wrote a long poem in his praise. Subsequently, when the media clouds had blown over, we were left to savour the acclaim of

[Who Said That?
JOHN BETJEMAN—NANCY SPAIN—JOANNA KILMARTIN
GILBERT HARDING

more well-disposed fellow poets like Philip Larkin.

Many writers since have tried to summarise Betjeman's achievement and to explain why his poetry should have such a great appeal for so many. The reasons are varied and complementary to one another. They way he wrote was generally clear but also adroit. He enjoyed being a 'rhymer' finding the exercise inspirational. Take a particularly adroit and perfectly orchestrated poem like *Middlesex* which he plunges into with:

> 'Gaily into Ruislip Gardens
>   Runs the red electric train,
> With a thousand Ta's and Pardon's
>   Daintily alights Elaine;

where the unobtrusive alliteration of 'daintily alights' hangs well with the well-nigh perfect name of 'Elaine' that he has chosen – first and foremost, of course, to rhyme with train. The poem is sent to the prestigious editor of *Punch* who brutally cuts out the whole of the second verse because it contains allusions to such commercial things as Windsmoor, Jacqmar, Drene and Innoxa simply because *Punch* could not allow such blatant advertising. The poem ends up intact in *A Few Late*

Chrysanthemums with its second verse full of advertisements and two further delicious verses of rural scene painting that justify the categorising of Middlesex, a now much-mangled county, as a 'rural Elysium'.

The primitive magic of rhyming has smitten even a poet like T. S. Eliot who, in a poem that must have greatly inspired Betjeman, breaks into his un-rhyming lines with a fanciful couplet like: 'In the room the women come and go Talking of Michelangelo' which perhaps more suitably to the period might have run,

> 'In the room the women never cease
> To chatter on the subject of Matisse.'

And Robert Browning, having hit on a splendid opening line like 'Oh, to be in England now that April's there', unwilling to forego such a catchy line bumbles along with 'And whoever wakes in England sees, some morning, unaware.' Unaware of what; how does anyone see unaware. What he means is perhaps sees 'unexpectedly' or 'unaware of what has happened' but grammatical sense has had to give way to the ruthlessness of rhyme.

Betjeman was a dab hand at manoeuvring his meaning toward the rhyme and the seemingly spontaneous thought that went with it that was going to fix the thought in memory for ever. As at the end of *The Hon.Sec.*

> '*The Times* would never have the space
> For Ned's discreet achievements;
> The public prints are not the place
> For intimate bereavements.
>
> A gentle guest, a willing host,
> Affection deeply planted
> It's strange that those we miss the most
> Are those we take for granted.'

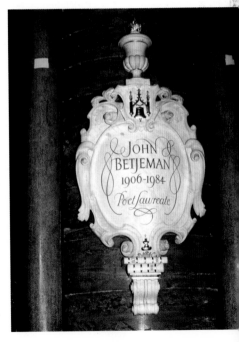

BELOW An elegant cartouche, wording designed by David Peace, installed in Poet's Corner, Westminster Abbey in 1996.

Bibliography

Books by Betjeman:
Poetry:

Mount Zion (James Press) [1931]

Continual Dew (John Murray) [1937][facsimile reprint 1977]

Old Lights for New Chancels (John Murray) [1940]

New Bats in Old Belfries (John Murray) [1945]

Selected Poems – edited by John Sparrow (John Murray) [1948]

A Few Late Chrysanthemums (John Murray) [1954]

Poems in the Porch (SPCK) [1954] [new expanded edition] [2008]

Pocket Poets: John Betjeman (Hulton Press) [1958]

Collected Poems – edited by Lord Birkenhead (John Murray) [1958]
[many reprints with the 2001 paperback the first to include *Uncollected Poems*
and the 2006 edition including *Summoned by Bells*]

Summoned by Bells (John Murray) [1960] Last reprinted [2007]
with Foreword by Griff Rhys Jones

A Ring of Bells – edited by Irene Slade. Illustrated Edward Ardizzone
(John Murray) [1963]

High and Low (John Murray) [1966]

A Nip in the Air (John Murray) [1974]

Church Poems (John Murray) [1980]

Uncollected Poems – edited by Bevis Hillier (John Murray) [1982]

The Illustrated Summoned by Bells – illustrated Hugh Casson (John Murray) [1989]

The Illustrated Poems of John Betjeman – illustrated David Gentleman
(John Murray) [1995]

Best Loved Poems of John Betjeman (John Murray) [2003]

Selected Poems – edited by Alan Powers. Illustrated Peter Baily
(Folio Society) [2004]

Faith and Doubt of John Betjeman (Continuum) [2005]

BIBLIOGRAPHY

Poetry and Prose:

Slick But Not Streamlined – edited by W. H. Auden
(Doubleday, New York) [1947]

The Best of Betjeman – edited by John Guest
(John Murray / Penguin Books) [1980]; new edition [2006]

Betjeman's Cornwall (John Murray) [1984]

Betjeman's London – edited by Pennie Denton
(John Murray) [1988]

Betjeman's Britain – edited by Candida Lycett Green
(Folio Society) [1999]

Prose:

Ghastly Good Taste (Chapman & Hall) [1933] [reprinted 1970]

An Oxford University Chest (John Miles) [1938] [reprinted 1970; 1979; 1990]

English Cities and Small Towns (Collins, 1943) [reprinted 1997]

First and Last Loves – edited by Myfanwy Piper (John Murray) [1952] [reprinted]

The City of London Churches (Pitkin) [1965] [reprinted 1995]

London's Historic Railway Stations (John Murray) [1972] [reprinted 2002]

Archie and the Strict Baptists – children's book (John Murray) [1977] [reprint 2006]

Letters, Volume One: 1926-1951 – edited by Candida Lycett Green (Methuen) [1994]

Letters, Volume Two: 1951-1984 – edited by Candida Lycett Green (Methuen) [1995]

Coming Home edited by Candida Lycett Green (Methuen) [1997]

John Betjeman on Trains edited by Jonathan Glancey (Methuen) [2006]

Trains and Buttered Toast: John Betjeman edited by Stephen Games (John Murray) [2006]

John Betjeman on Churches edited by Jonathan Glancey (Methuen) [2007]

Tennis Whites and Teacakes: John Betjeman edited by Stephen Games
(John Murray) [2007]

Sweet Songs of Zion: John Betjeman edited by Stephen Games (John Murray) [2007]

Betjeman's England: John Betjeman edited by Stephen Games (John Murray) [2009]

Books edited:

Collins Guide to English Parish Churches (Collins) [1958] [reprints]

English, Scottish and Welsh Landscape – with Geoffrey Taylor (Muller) [1944]

Altar and Pew: Church of England Verses (Hulton) [1959]

English Love Poems – with Geoffrey Taylor (Faber & Faber) [1964] [reprints]

The standard authorised Biography of Betjeman is the three-volume work by Bevis Hillier:

Vol.1 – *Young Betjeman* (1988; pbk.1989; new edition 2002; pbk.2003);
Vol.2 – *New Fame, New Love* (2002; pbk. 2003); Vol.3 – *The Bonus of Laughter* (2004; pbk. 2005). Published by John Murray. This is a magnificent monument to the poet and full of an incredible amount of detail both about him and the people who infringed on his life. No-one should be put off by its size or miss a chance to know virtually everything there is to know about the poet.

A condensed one-volume version was published in 2006.

A checklist compiled for its members by The Betjeman Society lists over 6,000 items written by and about the poet and they predict that there are still many more to be found. So there is plenty of available reading for those who care to search for it.

The Betjeman Society was founded in 1986 by Canterbury physiotherapist, Philippa Davies. She openly confesses that, having got into the Memorial Service in 1984 by saying she belonged to the Canterbury Betjeman Society, she soothed her conscience by forming the national society soon after. It hovers between 800 to 1,000 membership and has a lively programme of talks, visits and publications, including a yearly magazine *The Betjemanian* and a quarterly Newsletter. Presidents have been Lord Horder, Lady Wilson of Rievaulx and Bevis Hillier. Chairmen have been Philippa Davies, Peter Gammond, John Heald and David Pattison.

Membership enquiries should be addressed to:
Martin Revell
386 Hurst Road
Bexley
Kent DA5 3JI
www.johnbetjeman.com

Signed prints of John Ireland's drawing of Sir John Betjeman (opposite) are available via www.john-ireland.co.uk

**The pictures in this book were
provided courtesy of the following:**

GETTY IMAGES
101 Bayham Street, London NW1 0AG

EMPICS
www.empics.com

CORBIS
www.corbis.com

Candida Lycett Green and The Betjeman Estate
John Murray (Publishers) Ltd
Osbert Lancaster Estate
Jill Storer, Roger Woddis and the BBC
Mark Gerson, Ann Heald, Newsquest (Oxfordshire),
The Folio Society, Houghton Mifflin, Lippincott, Max Parrish
Faber & Faber, Oxford University Press, Hamish Hamilton, Doubleday,
SPCK, Charisma Records, John Murray
Daily Mail, Daily Express, Spectator, New Statesman, Punch, The Listener
Westminster Abbey, The Water Rats, Shell, David Engleheart,
Betjeman Centre Wadebridge, Thirties Society, Richard Cole, John Heald

Design and Artwork by David Wildish and Scott Giarnese

Published by G2 Entertainment Limited

Publishers Jules Gammond and Edward Adams

Written by Peter Gammond